Barry Ensign-George, Hélène Evers (Eds.)

Church Polity, Mission and Unity: Their Impact in Church Life

Church Polity and Ecumenism

Global Perspectives

edited by

Allan J. Janssen, Leo J. Koffeman,
Christina Landman, Johannes Smit
and C. Leon van den Broeke

Volume 5

LIT

Church Polity, Mission and Unity: Their Impact in Church Life

Proceedings of the International Conference, Princeton, New Jersey, USA, 18 – 20 April, 2016

edited by

Barry Ensign-George and Hélène Evers

LIT

This publication was made possible thanks to
The Presbyterian Foundation of the Presbyterian Church (USA) and
The Zonneweelde Foundation (Netherlands)

This book is printed on acid-free paper.

Bibliographic information published by the Deutsche Nationalbibliothek
The Deutsche Nationalbibliothek lists this publication in the Deutsche Nationalbibliografie; detailed bibliographic data are available in the Internet at http://dnb.dnb.de.

ISBN 978-3-643-90911-4 (pb)
ISBN 978-3-643-95911-9 (PDF)

A catalogue record for this book is available from the British Library.

Klosbachstr. 107
CH-8032 Zürich
Tel. +41 (0) 44-251 75 05
E-Mail: zuerich@lit-verlag.ch   http://www.lit-verlag.ch

Distribution:

In the UK: Global Book Marketing, e-mail: mo@centralbooks.com
In North America: Independent Publishers Group, e-mail: orders@ipgbook.com
In Germany: LIT Verlag Fresnostr. 2, D-48159 Münster
Tel. +49 (0) 2 51-620 32 22, Fax +49 (0) 2 51-922 60 99, e-mail: vertrieb@lit-verlag.de
e-books are available at www.litwebshop.de

Table of Contents

PREFACE

What are the connections between the polity of the church and church unity – or division? Does the polity of churches serve or obstruct the missional nature of the church? These questions were the focus of the Third Conference of the International Protestant Church Polity Study Group (IPCPSG), held in Princeton, New Jersey in April 2016. The authors of the essays that follow probe these questions from a variety of angles.

There was, as well, another question at play. The Conference was held in the United States, a place where Protestants have a strong tendency to view polity as only indirectly a theological matter. As one of the contributors notes in his first paragraph, "[U]se of church order and polity are often viewed as, at best, necessary evils in pastoral work. Regrettably, this aspect of ministry has received far too little theological attention" (see below, Griswold). One purpose of the Conference, a purpose that finds expression in this volume, was to model close attention to and reflection on the theological import and value of church order and polity, especially for those who assume polity has little theological import. Polity is always theologically laden, as the authors of the following papers demonstrate.

Attendees of the conference came from churches and denominations in the Reformed tradition, gathering from across the United States and around the world. Attendees included scholars of church order and polity, and practitioners with depth of knowledge and experience gained through the exercise of polity in a variety of settings and contexts. Conference papers, discussions, and informal conversations turned from theological reflection to practice in particular cases and back to theological reflection again.

The series to which the third conference and this volume belong

The conference was the third conference of the IPCPSG. The first was held in Utrecht, the Netherlands, 7–10 November, 2011. The theme was Protestant Church Polity in Changing Contexts. The second was held in Pretoria, South Africa, 24–27 March, 2014. The theme of this conference was Good Governance in Church and Society Today. This conference produced no published material. The essays in this present collection are from the third conference in Princeton.

Papers from or related to these conferences have been published by LIT-Verlag in the Church Polity and Ecumenism: Global Perspectives series. First in the series is *In Order to Serve: An Ecumenical Introduction to Church Polity*, by Leo J. Koffeman. That is followed by two volumes of papers given at the first conference: *Protestant Church Polity in Changing Contexts, Vol. I: Ecclesiological and Historical Contributions*, edited by Allan J. Janssen and Leo J. Koffeman and *Protestant Church Polity in Changing Contexts, Vol. II: Case Studies*, edited by Leo J. Koffeman and Johannes Smit. Fourth in the series is *The Protestant Church in the Netherlands: Church Unity in the 21st Century: Stories and Reflections*, edited by Arjan Plaisier and Leo J. Koffeman. All four of these volumes were published in 2014. Fifth in the series is the present volume.

The papers in this volume

The papers that follow in this volume are gathered in two groups. First come three papers that explore polity, mission, and unity from a distinctly theological angle. Second, there follows a group of papers that explore these issues by highlighting particular situations in which polity, mission, and unity impact the life of the church.

There are three papers in the first group. Daniel M. Griswold draws on the long theological reflection of the threefold office of Jesus Christ, and on the idea of *perichoresis* in the doctrine of the Trinity to deepen our understanding of church order as an embodiment of basic theological understandings. Hélène Evers tackles the basic question, why church order? She draws on the work of legal scholar Paul Scholten in shaping an answer. The answer she offers provides the basis for a polity tool kit for missional communities. Allan J. Janssen probes the role of 'broader assemblies – classes/presbyteries and synods' in the church. He proposes that assemblies are secondary to congregations in the church, supporting congregations as they seek to live ever more fully their identity.

There are nine papers in the second group. They deal with the church in France, Indonesia, the Netherlands, South Africa, and the United States. Herman Speelman tells the story of ecclesial unity and differentiation in Reformation-era France. He notes a time in which the governing authorities legitimated the existence of more than one church within its realm – an early instance of denominations. Roy Alexander Surjanegara explores Indonesian understandings of life together, showing how they support the call to unity in the church.

Three papers explore the shape and exercise of church polity in the Netherlands. Leo J. Koffeman focuses on the de-christianizing context of the church in the Netherlands. He considers traditional marks of church unity, particularly agreement in doctrine. He claims that agreement in doctrine is the primary source of denominational identity and differentiation. He suggests that this mark of unity is fading away, leading to a post-denominational church whose polity can contain diverging views on doctrine and worship practice. Klaas-Willem De Jong examines cases in which the decision of a governing body of the Protestant Church in the Netherlands is appealed. He notes that such cases are generally settled in ways that downplay the theological claims often implicit in such appeals. De Jong proposes an alternative that allows recognition of the role of theological convictions in such appeals. Finally, Leon Van den Broeke sees the rise of missional ecclesiologies as marking a fundamental turn in the church's self-understanding. He proposes a 'missional Reformed church polity' that better serves the missional identity of the church.

The next two papers explore the situation of Reformed churches and denominations in South Africa. Leepo Modise and Basimane Makoko's paper explores the long effort to reunite Reformed denominations that were separated on the basis of race. They lift up the central importance of the Confession of Belhar's insistence that separation on the basis of race among Christians and the structures in which they gather is sin. The authors lay out the way in which the denominations involved continue to embody the racial segregations central to apartheid. They critique the DRC for its unwillingness to override parts of its polity in pursuit of denominational reunion aimed at visibly rejecting apartheid and its legacy. Next, Nelus Niemandt, like Klaas-Willem De Jong, considers the way in which polity can obstruct the living out of the missional nature of the church. Looking specifically at the DRC, Niemandt proposes that the commitment of that denomination to being fully missional will require that its polity be revised to serve that end.

Finally, two papers explore polity, mission, and unity in the context of Reformed denominations in the United States. Kathy Smith seeks to clarify why church polity is necessary, how it serves church unity and mission, how it helps to clarify situations of disunity, and how a dynamic polity can help the church engage in mission with flexibility and responsiveness. Smith suggests that the books of polity are similar to the Bible's wisdom literature. She identifies ways in which her own denomination, the Christian Reformed Church in North America has demonstrated the power of polity to hold Christians together. Clyde Steckel studies the history of polity in the United Church of Christ (UCC), lifting up its turn to covenant as a way of understanding its polity. Steckel identifies ways in which this understanding of polity undergirds efforts by the UCC and its congregations to live out the missional identity and ecumenical imperative of the church.

Gratitude

This volume and the conference on which it is based came to be through the support of multiple individuals and institutions.

The Conference was organized by Leo J. Koffeman, Allan J. Janssen, Hélène Evers, Joseph D. Small, and Barry A. Ensign-George.

Publication of this volume has been underwritten by generous financial support from the Presbyterian Foundation of the Presbyterian Church (U.S.A.) and the Zonneweelde foundation in the Netherlands. Both provided support for the conference itself. The organizers of the conference wish to thank both institutions for their generous support. The Erdman Center of Princeton Theological Seminary provided a welcoming, comfortable setting for the Conference. The staff there was reliably helpful. The conference organizers are very grateful for both facilities and staff.

The organizers recognize the stimulating role of Leo J. Koffeman in making this publication possible. They are also grateful to LIT-Verlag for its work on this volume, as on previous volumes published as part of the work of the International Protestant Church Polity Study Group.

GOVERNING THE CHURCH: A THEOLOGICAL REFLECTION ON CHURCH ORDER

Daniel M. Griswold

Church order often gets a bad rap. Use of church order and polity are often viewed as, at best, necessary evils in pastoral work. Regrettably, this aspect of ministry has received far too little theological attention.

Along with its cousin, church administration, church order is widely perceived as remote or even antithetical to 'real' pastoral concerns. Those who do find value in church polity know that their interests are not widely shared. They have grown accustomed to being viewed by others as at best engaging in a strange and irrelevant hobby, or as being insufficiently spiritual, pastoral, or missional. Such is the peculiar burden of 'polity nerds'.

To be fair, some ministers find the details of a church's polity overwhelming. For some, they experience it as an ever-shifting game of 'gotcha' played against them by sly adepts, a game they can never win. They see church order as a realm of congregational and denominational reality for which they feel particularly unsuited by virtue of training and natural giftedness. On the former, who can blame them, as church order endured almost complete neglect within the curriculum of most North American seminaries until recently.

So, a felt dichotomy of polity and the pastoral is understandable, as is a rejection of church order. I would argue, however, that the solution to the difficulties with polity is not the rejection of church order as a valid pastoral responsibility. Rather, the solution may be found in a more adequate theological understanding of the nature of church order.

I propose to do just that: to consider church order theologically. Here I will advance a theological understanding of pastoral church governance. I will draw on resources found within the broad Christian theological tradition, as well as some specifically from the Reformed theological tradition.

Munus triplex in the Reformed tradition

It is with that Reformed tradition that I begin, namely, with a Christological motif characteristic of, but not unique to, classical Reformed theology: that of the *munus triplex*, or the threefold office of Christ, who was and is prophet, priest, and king. The *munus triplex* is deployed in the tradition as a tool for summarizing and describing the work of Jesus Christ.

In the words of John Calvin, "the office enjoined upon Christ by the Father consists of three parts. For he was given to be prophet, king, and priest" (Calvin 1559, II.XV.1). To be sure, that understanding of the work of Christ had a provenance before Calvin, but thereafter it became a common feature in Reformed theology. To address Christ's work under the headings of Prophet, Priest, and King was seen in Reformed circles as appropriate and useful. The Heidelberg Catechism, a Reformed document from the late 16th century, contains an especially important example:

Q. Why is he called 'Christ,' meaning anointed?

A. Because he has been ordained by God the Father and has been anointed with the Holy Spirit to be our chief *prophet* and teacher who perfectly reveals to us the secret counsel and will of God for our redemption; our only *high priest* who has redeemed us by the one sacrifice of his body, and who continually pleads our cause with the Father; and our eternal *king* who governs us by his Word and Spirit, and who guards us and keeps us in the redemption he has won for us. (HC, q&a 31; emph. added).

In short, according to this part of the catechism, as prophet Christ *reveals* to us, as priest he *redeems* us, and as king he *governs* us. Revelation, redemption, and governance are three primary ways in which Jesus Christ acts.

The implications of the *munus triplex* have traditionally been fairly well developed in the areas of Christology (the doctrine of the person and work of Jesus Christ) and soteriology (the doctrine of salvation). Less attention has been given to the implications of the threefold office for ecclesiology (the doctrine of the nature of the church), although some connections are apparent in both Roman Catholic and Protestant traditions. The lack of attention is regrettable, for there are important implications of the *munus triplex* for how we understand the church and our role in it, and, in particular, church office and pastoral leadership.

A helpful direction for filling that void may be pursued if we follow the Heidelberg Catechism to the very next question and answer, No. 32:

Q. But why are you called a Christian?

A. Because by faith I am a member of Christ and so I *share in his anointing*. I am anointed to confess his name, to present myself to him as a living sacrifice of thanks, to strive with a good conscience against sin and the devil in this life, and afterward to reign with Christ over all creation for all eternity. (HC, q&a 32; emph. added).

Granted, the *munus triplex* is present here only implicitly. However, this entry of the Catechism says that Christians share in the anointing of Christ, who, as was said in the immediately preceding entry of the Catechism, was anointed to be prophet, priest, and king. It is an intriguing connection. But the Catechism offers no development of the implications of this 'sharing'. Could there be a way of developing these implications?

To be sure, in q&a 31, with regard to Christ himself, the *munus triplex* is itself merely a hint. That hint necessarily leads to many questions. Of what does Christ's prophetic work consist? What effect does it have? And what of the priestly work of intercession, not only with regard to the Christian's salvation but also her discipleship? What practical import is there to Christ's royal work of ruling and governance?

One finds in the Catechism only hints: that the work of Christ may be understood along certain lines, and that we, somehow, share in that work, inasmuch as we share in his anointing. Nevertheless, q&a 31 does use the *munus triplex*, and q&a 32 does suggest a connection of the believer with the threefold anointing of Christ. Can that suggested connection be fruitfully explored?

I believe it can, but to do that requires one more preliminary step, namely, to highlight the kind of action envisioned in q&a 31. Is Christ's work merely in the past? Surely, it is not. With the Spirit, Christ 'has been' anointed, as Prophet, Priest, and King. But the work he does in these roles is both past and present. He 'reveals to us'. He 'has redeemed us' and yet 'continually pleads our cause with the Father'. He 'governs us … and … guards us and keeps us'. Clearly, Christ's work is present, and not just past, because Jesus Christ is risen from the dead, and 'is seated at the right hand of God the Father almighty'. Through the Holy Spirit, the ascended Christ remains the anointed Christ. And through the Spirit his threefold office is effective even now, for the Risen One continues to be Prophet, Priest, and King, whose work is continued on earth through the work of that same Spirit. Jesus Christ is the Risen, Anointed One. As *risen*, he continues, through the Holy Spirit, to guide and bless the church through his ongoing prophetic, priestly, and royal activity, for his *anointing* continues to this day in his work of prophecy, intercession, and governance. The church, as the body of Christ, by the Holy Spirit shares in Christ's anointing, and so shares in Christ's work, which is always prophetic, priestly, and royal. Indeed, when the church truly is the body of Christ, the work it does is truly the work of Christ, for the gifts that the Spirit of Christ bestows on the people of God are given to manifest the ministry of Christ. We might well recall Ephesians 4 here: "But each of us was given grace according to the measure of Christ's gift.... The gifts he gave were that some would be apostles, some prophets, some evangelists, some pastors and teachers, to equip the saints for the work of ministry, for building up the body of Christ" (Ephesians 4:7, 11–12, NRSV).

Christians, then, are connected to Christ's anointing because his anointing and his anointed work continue even now, and furthermore because the Holy Spirit joins them to that work through the various gifts Christ gives them to participate in that work.

The royal office

So now let's focus more specifically on the royal office in Christ's anointing, with an eye toward what this means for how the church participates in Christ's anointing. In that regard, we might ask two questions: 'What does the royal office mean?' and 'What might a sharing in that anointed work of Christ mean?'.

First: what does the royal office mean? A short answer to that question is easily stated: The royal office means that, as King, Christ continues through the Holy Spirit to govern the church — guiding its ministry, guarding its existence, correcting its people, ordering its common life, leading its conflict against the kingdom of darkness. More, however, must be said. For that royal work is often understood in individualistic terms, namely, with regard to the spiritual state of individual Christians (this seems to be the case also with q&as 31 and 32 of the Heidelberg Catechism.) But that is a regrettably limited understanding of Christ's royal work. While the governance Christ exercises as King is certainly a spiritual governance with respect to individuals, it must not be understood as exclusively individual. Nor is it to be understood as 'spiritual' in the sense of having no bearing on the way in which members of the church really live out their discipleship with each other and in the world. Eugene Petersen's *Christ Plays in Ten-Thousand Places* is a fine counterweight to corrupt and vacuous understandings of spirituality (cf. Petersen 2005).

Christ rules not merely individual Christians. Christ rules the church, the body of Christ, the communion of saints. From a scriptural point of view, this is more than merely a gathering of like-minded individuals (which, it must be said, is often the extent of congregations' self-understanding).

We can turn now to the second question, 'What might a sharing in that anointed work of Christ mean?' Here, our answer to this question recognizes the corporate implications and the practical possibilities of Christ's royal office. What might a sharing in the specifically royal office of Christ's anointing mean? Surely, it might mean an enhanced (or even altered) understanding of church governance and polity. When church leaders engage in their leadership out of the conviction that Christ rules the church, as well as the conviction that their leadership can and must participate in that rule, then we find enhanced not only church polity (the rules and procedures by which the church is governed) but even church administration (the practices by which the activities of the church are organized and put into effect). Indeed, if we truly believe that members of the body of Christ share in Christ's anointing, and that Christ was anointed to be prophet, priest, and king, then the implication seems clear: members of the body of Christ share in his work of governance.

The implications are profound. This governance that the church exercises as empowered by the Spirit of Jesus, contrary to some ways of understanding it, is a truly spiritual activity. To share in Christ's royal office, in terms of church polity, is to do holy work. Church order is so much more than knowledge of arcane rules. It is, or is supposed to be, an important means by which the ministry of the church actually happens. As so many pastors and other church leaders know from sad experience, good intentions are not enough. For ministry to happen, order must, at least provisionally, prevail over chaos, and light must, to some extent, dispel darkness. The work of church order is a sharing in Christ's anointed work of governance, by which he brings order out of chaos and light out of darkness.

Yet it is always a *sharing* in Christ's anointing, and thus a sharing in his work. Never do we come to acquire the anointing as our own, or possess the work as our own, either as individuals or as the church of Jesus Christ. The governance of the church fails to be Christ's royal work when individuals or institutions come to believe that this work is exclusively their own, by power or privilege or right. No one member of the body has an exclusive lock on the role of governance, admitting no others. Even in those forms of polity in which governance is seen as the distinct responsibility of the ordained, that responsibility is always shared with others, both those who are ordained and, perhaps in different ways, even with those who are not.

This, of course, is a temptation to which ministers frequently succumb. They easily adopt a 'clerical mindset', which divides the church into leaders and followers, those few (typically the ministers, or, at the denominational level, certain members of the national staff) who govern and those many who are governed. Allan Janssen helpfully warns of the dangers of a 'clerocracy' (see Janssen 2000, 47).

Besides being a failure of theological vision, this mindset leads to a host of practical problems in the church. In our own day, a great problem is burnout of pastors and other church leaders. For once a pastor accepts the proposition that only ministers are called to govern the church, then that individual has set out on a lonely road that never ends and is full of peril. For that pastor has accepted as fact the theologically bankrupt notion that nobody can do this work but the pastor.

Yet the danger to the individual pastor is not the only problem with this temptation. The damage to congregations this notion can inflict may be just as great, if not greater. For the clerical mindset tends to hinder the members of the body from exercising the gifts the Spirit of Christ has given to them for building up the body. It places obstacles in the way of those whom Christ chooses, from time to time, to be the instruments of his royal, governing work. It tends to make congregations dependent on their pastors, which is inimical to true spiritual growth. When the pastor leaves, whether because of a call to a different church or retirement or death, what is the congregation to do?

This is an important lesson for pastors to learn. The work of church governance, if it truly is to be a sharing in Christ's anointing as King, must be exercised humbly and collaboratively by those entrusted with it. The burdens of governance must be shared: for the good of ministers, for the good of the congregations they serve, and for integrity to the one we all serve, the one Head of the Church, Jesus Christ. It is in this respect, and in this alone, that church office is to be understood as functional: in terms of the tasks to which Christ call his servants, and in the exercising of which they are obedient to his call.

As Christians, we share in Christ's anointing. Again, this has implications for church order, for we share in Christ's anointing as King, and thus we share in his royal work of governing the church. Yet another lesson for church leaders may be learned. This lesson is that just as one cannot understand Christ as king without also understanding him as prophet and priest, so too one cannot understand Christ's royal office (in which we participate) in isolation from his prophetic and priestly offices (in which we likewise have a share). Thus the church must learn that polity must not be treated in isolation from the prophetic and priestly work of Jesus in which the church also must share, because such isolation betrays a profound misunderstanding, not only of church order, but even more so of the nature of what *kind* of king Christ was and is: who leads by dying, whose royal path goes straight through Gethsemane, Golgotha, and Gehenna.

In such isolation, church governance easily becomes process for process's sake, the tyranny of rules, the bureaucratization of the church. For it forgets that its purpose is to organize and make effective our presentation of the grace of Christ, his gift and task, the priestly intercession and the prophetic challenge. Without the prophetic and priestly offices informing and energizing it, church order becomes merely the soul-deadening maintenance of an institution of dubious relevance. Without a clear understanding of the nature of this King we serve, even in our governance in his name, then we are no longer bringing order out of chaos or light to dispel the darkness, but rather imposing our own chaos and spreading our own darkness. Church order ceases to be true to Christ, who is head of the church, when it is no longer the work of Christ, who is not only King but also

Prophet and Priest. At all points, church order must reflect not only the discipline of Christ who rules us, but also the revelation of the Good News of that same Christ as prophet, and the intercession of that same Christ who is our high priest. Church governance must honor Jesus Christ, who in his earthly ministry embraced sinners, challenged the powerful, and often seemed quite disdainful of rules. The embrace, challenge, and freedom of this same Christ continues, as he is risen, and so he must be honored as risen by any church governance that claims his name.

What is needed, then, in this practical application of the *munus triplex* is a healthy dose of *perichoresis* (cf. Griswold 2015, particularly chapters 5 and 7).

Perichoresis

In contemporary discussions of the doctrine of the Trinity, the Greek notion of *perichoresis* ('to dance around') has been revived to express the conviction that the different persons of the Godhead never operate in isolation from each other, but that their work is always in cooperation with and among each other: the Father in the Son and through the Holy Spirit, the Son blessed by the Father and conveyed through the Spirit, the Spirit of the Son sent by the Father. Perhaps this sleight of hand can allow me to avoid the whole filioque controversy for now. But if not, then I ask forgiveness from those who might be offended by my all too Western, or perhaps for some insufficiently Western, construction.

Such 'dialectical inclusion', as George Hunsinger calls it (cf. Hunsinger 1991, 85–86, 107–109), is much what I am after with the *munus triplex*. The three offices must be understood, not in isolation from each other, but in connection, each of them including the others. The royal, prophetic, and priestly offices dialectically include each other, mutually enriching and defining each other for our benefit. The same must be said of the works of those offices: the work of governance, the work of prophecy, the work of priestly intercession. Moreover, the perichoretic or dialectically inclusive relationship between these offices and thus between their works applies not only when they are exercised by Christ, who is anointed for these offices and works, but also when we share in them, inasmuch as we have a share in Christ's own anointing.

This is all to say that true church governance must be prophetic and priestly. Those who engage in church governance must allow to have full effect the prophetic and priestly work that the church undertakes in the name of Jesus. Such applies even to the governance of the church in its specifically administrative form. Those who organize and plan the work of the church should be encouraged that their work is not 'merely administrative'.

Rather, their work can, may, and must be directed to the proclamation of the gospel of grace, the declaration of Christ's gracious call to follow him, and his challenge to leave behind all that would hinder our following (the prophetic); as well as to the making plain the way to God, the alleviation of suffering, and the healing of the ill (the priestly). In all these, this holy work is done in the name of him in whose anointing we have a share. At the same time, the perichoretic nature of the work of the church serves an important guiding function as church leaders operate within the bounds of their church polity. For it reminds us of the values that should inform church governance. In our day, church leadership, not only at the local but certainly also at the denominational level, frequently adopts values that have little to do with the Christ who is not only King but also Prophet and Priest. As important as values such as efficiency, productivity, popularity, or power may be in other endeavors, they are not the values that should be determinative for the church. The values of the church should be those learned from the Lord of the Church, who was and remains Prophet, Priest, and King.

But the dialectical inclusion works in the other direction, as well. Those who are most passionate about the prophetic or the priestly aspects of the church's work must not reject the governance function of the church. For church governance, through polity and administration, is the means by which the church organizes and makes effective the works that may be considered prophetic or priestly. Indeed, governance is the *form* in which the Spirit-enabled works of the church, insofar as they are also prophetic and priestly, are embodied or given shape.

Conclusion

It is quite common to find pastors and other church workers who dismiss the structures and guides of church order as unnecessary obstacles to their important work. And to be sure, bureaucratic nonsense is a problem in many congregations and denominations. However, a healthy understanding of the practical and theological necessity for church order should lead to practical and theologically rich structures for enabling the work of the church.

The work that pastors and other church leaders are called to do is at times difficult and complex. Many factors affect the complexity: competing expectations of ministers, ministry, and congregations; varied cultural contexts; varieties of gifts and abilities. It is easy, and common, for that complexity to be addressed, forcibly, by adopting simplistic understandings of the nature of church leadership. Such a reaction typically does damage to church leaders and congregations alike. What is needed is a theologically deep understanding of the nature of church leadership, one that honors our risen and anointed Lord who remains Prophet, Priest, and King, in whose anointing the body of Christ is blessed to share.

Abbreviations and bibliography

HC: Heidelberg Catechism
NRSV: New Revised Standard Version

Calvin, John. 1559. Institutes of the Christian Religion. Two volumes. Edited by John T. McNeill. Translation Ford Lewis Battles 1960. Philadelphia: The Westminster Press – London: SCM.

Griswold, Daniel M. 2015. Triune Eternality: God's Relationship to Time in the Theology of Karl Barth. Emerging Scholars. Minneapolis: Fortress Press.

Hunsinger, George. 1991. How to Read Karl Barth: The Shape of His Theology. New York: Oxford University Press.

Janssen, Allan J. 2000. Constitutional Theology: Notes on the Book of Church Order of the Reformed Church in America. Grand Rapids, MI: Eerdmans.

Petersen, Eugene H. 2005. Christ Plays in Ten-Thousand Places: A Conversation in Spiritual Theology. Grand Rapids, MI: Eerdmans.

PAUL SCHOLTEN'S VIEWS ON THE INDISPENSABILITY OF A CHURCH ORDER

Hélène Evers

1. Mission and Church polity

In this contribution, I will take a close look at the necessity for each church to have a church polity or church order. I will explain why this is necessary not only for existing churches, but also for missionary initiatives. Therefore, I will use the thoughts of an eminent Dutch Law Professor, Paul Scholten. He was able to make his thoughts fruitful for the Netherlands Reformed Church and they were of great importance for the church order of the Protestant Church in the Netherlands of today. I will try to show how his understanding can also be fruitful for missionary initiatives around the world now.

I would like to help missionary initiatives, their longing for sustainability, to become a church or a Christian community, by applying the lessons in the area of church polity that older churches have learned through the ages. We should help them rather than ignoring them. How can we, as academics, make our expertise and interest in polity fruitful for the mission of our church and for missionary initiatives of other churches or private organizations as well? At the end of this contribution I add an appendix containing a simple tool kit that might be helpful in building a sustainable community.

At the outset, most initiators of missionary activities will not be interested in church polity or church law. They are naturally focused on the work of an evangelist. However, when the work expands and people are interested in the gospel of Jesus Christ, a community arises. This is the work of the Holy Spirit, who always connects people and brings people into a community.

It is at this point that the necessity of church law becomes relevant: in sustaining the community. This is what we must make clear to the initiators of missionary activities and where we can offer a helping hand.

In this contribution, I hope to describe these basics clearly, and explain the necessity of church law. I hope this will serve the mission of the church, as well as the church itself. I hope both will serve the Body of Christ.

2. Introducing Paul Scholten

I learned a lot about these matters from Paul Scholten. He was one of the major Dutch scholars of law at the University of Amsterdam. I would like to introduce him and his thinking to academic church law scholars internationally. The keynote of Scholten's teaching is that the necessity for the church to have church polity/order is rooted *both* in the origin, the character, the essence of what the church is,*and* in the origin, the character or the essence of law, order and justice.

Let me give a short biography of Paul Scholten (1875–1946). He was professor at the Faculty of law at the University of Amsterdam. He taught various subjects. His most famous work, the *General Method of Private Law*, discusses an overarching subject that concerns all parts of civil law, namely method. He taught the lawyer to reflect on his method and so he taught what law actually is. Nowadays there is a digital English translation available at www.paulscholten.eu. There Paul Scholten is introduced as 'one of the most important legal theorists in the Netherlands'. The book which has brought him this fame, the Algemeen Deel (General Part), was written in 1931. This book consists of three chapters and the first chapter on the method of private law (179 pages) is the primary source for Paul Scholten's fame today. A striking characteristic of this chapter is that it is written from the perspective of the judge.

For many Dutch jurists the chapter on the method of private law is a relevant source, for which they find no equivalent in the international body of knowledge. It was translated into French in 1954 and the whole book (Algemeen Deel/General Part) into Indonesian in 1992. Nowadays, however, English has become the lingua franca for the whole world. Therefore, it is important for Dutch legal theorists that the chapter on the method of private law has been translated into English and is published in Open Access.

Scholten was not involved in the church when he was younger, but that changed after his conversion at the age of 38 (in 1913). In his opinion, law and philosophy of life cannot be separated. Since then his Christian philosophy resonated in his legal work. He became more and more involved in the church. From 1931, he was a member of several reorganization committees of the Netherlands Reformed Church that examined how the law of the church could best fit the essence of the church. In 1940, he became an elder of the Netherlands Reformed Church in Amsterdam.

In 1940, at the outbreak of the Second World War, he became involved in the resistance against the German occupation. Most particularly, the battle had to be fought against Nazism in people's minds. When his son, G.J. Scholten, who had been actively fighting south of Rotterdam as a soldier, met his father again for the first time, Scholten said to him "Till now you have done it, now it is our time". By this he meant that after the frustrated military attempts by soldiers to defeat the enemy, now the mental battle against National Socialism had to begin. Scholten did this both openly and in underground resistance.

Scholten became one of the leaders of spiritual resistance in the Netherlands, especially in the churches and the universities. At the University of Amsterdam, he was the leader of the protest against the introduction of the so-called 'Ariër-paragraaf' [Arian paragraph]. This paragraph was part of the Nuremberg Racial Laws. The German occupying authority forced students and academic teachers to sign a declaration that they were 'of the Arian race', i.e. not Jewish. This was devised to mark Jewish students and professors, and later to deny them access to the universities.

Scholten also spoke to the occupying authorities on behalf of the Netherlands Reformed Church. He was a danger to the Germans and therefore he was fired by them in 1942. He was banned from the university and forced to live in the countryside in The Netherlands, far away from Amsterdam and the centre of the academic world.

After the liberation of the country in 1945, he made himself available to the Dutch Government for the task of the purging officials of the judiciary. He died in 1946. Many have appreciated the fact that Scholten shaped his lifestyle to his faith.

3. The essence of Law

"Law is both the government-imposed law, the norm expressing the authority that maintains it, *and* the people's behavior according to the rules that prevail within a nation and that develop naturally from such behavior. Law is part of our spiritual life, the collective spirit ... ultimately it is rooted in the division of good and evil. In this, man reaches above himself, from the law that is bound to the social organization and to the judgment of the community under law, to a higher justice that he always longs for, and from which he remains ever separated, since he is sinful and forever falling short" (Scholten 1949, 503).

Scholten makes clear that law is more than the written law given by the law-giver. We call the latter legal positivism: the written law decides what is just. In the 19th century in the Netherlands legal positivism was the usual view of law. In the 20th century it was realized that this view is far too limited, and that justice exists outside the law as well. In the end, legal positivism was abandoned. In the Netherlands, legal thinking developed towards the justice positivism that Scholten describes above, when he says that law is ultimately rooted in the difference between good and evil. He has contributed to this development.

It is noticeable that many theologians approach church law with the limited view of legal positivism: the written rules alone decide what is right. During the process of reorganizing Netherlands Reformed Church law, Scholten attempted to teach theologians the nature of the law. He tried to make it clear that justice needs to be found in the law of the church, but that the rules in themselves, the articles of church law, do not ultimately define what is just. Furthermore, he contributed to the phrasing of the articles of church law, stating in the text of the articles what makes the church a church and what is her function and purpose. He did not want to leave this to the Confession of Faith but wished to include it also in the text of the Church Order.

It is essential that law, including church law, concerns an organizing of the relationship of one person to the other with whom he lives in a community. Scholten: "Law is the arrangement of the relationships between human beings living together. It applies to a particular group, a community" (Scholten 1949, 72). We can participate in multiple communities, for example the community of the company, of the family, the school and the community of the church. The community based on the rule by the people (a nation) is often the most predominant.

This is an important argument for the necessity of law in building a stable community. Law arranges the relationships. Without law you cannot have community. "Law aims at peace". "In a society of poor, sinful people, who are capable of all sorts of evil, a decision given by authorities does not always bring peace. Yet the aim of the law is peace. Not the peace which passes all understanding, but poor earthly peace, which leaves the other person in peace" (Scholten 1949, 61).

For Scholten the Christian faith and Christian love are the necessary foundation of any legal idea. Man cannot autonomously put himself under any obligation; behind every command, every authority there has to be a person. That is why according to Scholten, we cannot understand the authority of the law if the relationship of man to God is not its foundation. Another function of the law is that it limits the power of the State and the authority of the Government, because there is a higher power, God.

4. The essence of church

To establish that church law is essential for the church and indispensable in developing missionary initiatives into stable churches or faith communities, it must be shown that churches are essentially also communities of people. Paul Scholten has helped the Netherlands Reformed Church to search for and find her identity and to put this into words, and he strove to give her a form that fits her identity. He did this during the thirties and forties of the 20th century, presiding over several reorganization committees, and finally as president of the Commission of principles for Church order (1942–1944). This last commission formulated a number of principles that describe what a church essentially is.

4.1. The visibility of the Una Sancta

The first principle they formulated was that the visible church is part of the essence of the invisible church, the *Una Sancta.* This implies an analysis of the relationship between the visible and the invisible church that says that the visible church is a manifestation of the invisible church. In this analysis, there is only one church, not two, a visible and an invisible one. Both are aspects of the same church. This manifestation is part of the essence of the invisible church, the one, holy, catholic, Christian church, the *Una Sancta.*

So, on the one hand, the church is what we believe it is. As Scholten said: "Treat her as if she is truly church, that is to say, remember that, whatever you say and do to and about her, she is – whatever she is in practice – yet she is the church that we believe she is according to the Apostolic Confession: the holy catholic church, *sanctam ecclesiam catholicam.* And the Order of the church is a true system of law; theologians who deny this do not realize what law is" (Herdenkingsnummer, 479).

On the other hand, the church is not just an article of faith. It is also visible. We find this view of the manifest church, e.g. with Calvin. Therefore, we can say that this view is the opposite of saying that the church is essentially invisible. This last view was held by Luther, and we meet it again in Rudolph Sohm (1841–1917), a German Lutheran jurist. His is the well-known quote, "Das Wesen der Kirche ist geistlich" (the essence of the church is spiritual). A different view of the church leads to a different view of church law. This led to Sohm's best-known statement: "Das Kirchenrecht steht mit dem Wesen der Kirche im Widerspruch" (Church law is a contradiction of the essence of church). (Sohm 1892, 1). So, for churches and missionary initiatives it is extremely important to decide what they consider to be the essence of the church. For Sohm church and law were mutually exclusive: "Das Wesen der Kirche ist geistlich. Das Wesen des Rechts ist weltlich" (the essence of the church is spiritual; the essence of law is secular.)

Scholten opposes Rudolph Sohm (Oostenbrink-Evers 2000, 93). According to Scholten's understanding of the church, the invisible church must become visible in the empirical church. His efforts in the area of church organization were grounded in his conviction that the visible aspect of the church is an essential part of the church in this dispensation. The actions of the visible church are linked with the invisible church. Therefore, he considered it the duty of the church to have the best possible church order (Oostenbrink-Evers 2000, 91). "The church has a special significance. Yet as far as she is defined as a community of believers she needs law to order the life of this community of believers" (Oostenbrink-Evers

2000, 3). Scholten demonstrates that the church as a community of people cannot exist without law.

4.2. Community

For the church, it is fundamental that she is a meeting, a community of Christian believers. The church is a community of people who expect their salvation from Jesus Christ, yet at the same time they remain sinful people. Therefore, Scholten says, "It is the tragedy of the history of the church that no lasting community of any substantial size can survive without polity. If anywhere, then in purely spiritual things, domination should be excluded: the power of one person over another should be banned. Nevertheless, church history teaches us that every community – if she does not want to fade or evaporate and thereby dissolve itself – needs outward boundaries and inward regulations and hence a law and upholding of that law by appointed people. Rudolph Sohm is entirely right when he announces that 'church' and 'law' exclude each other, but it is equally true that a church, if she is serious in excluding every law and all maintenance of the law, will inevitably break down" (Scholten 1949, 192).

'No community life without law'. This statement applies not only in history, but also in the very substance of finite, sinful people, who cannot avoid clashing. It is Scholten's belief that legal forms, also in the church, always have a double purpose to consolidate and capture what is, and to offer the possibility to create new developments.

5. Essential elements in Church Law

Starting from the essence of the empirical church, i.e. the manifestation of the *Una Sancta*, Scholten develops a number of essential elements in the empirical church. In this he differs from theologians who advocate a purely functional church order. In Scholten's day, this position was defended by Bakhuizen van den Brink (Oostenbrink-Evers 2000, 95), whose view of the church was comparable to Sohm's.

I encounter this view today as well, for instance among students at the Evangelical Theology Faculty in Louvain, who generally come from free evangelical churches. In their reactions to my lectures, they initially come up with thoughts such as 'A few practical guidelines ought to be enough to order the church'. Such thinking ignores the notion of the relationship between the visible, empirical church and the Una Sancta.

Again, Scholten does not share this view. Because he recognizes an essential link between the Una Sancta and the empirical church, he investigates the implications of this view for the shape and structure of the empirical church. Not just any law will fit the church. There is a connection between the essence of the character of the church and the essence of the character of law.

A church order defines the shape of the church of Jesus Christ. (Balke and Oostenbrink-Evers 1995, 175). Not every form/shape suits this content. The shape must be appropriate to the content. Underlying every system of law there is a ruling idea that determines its shape and application. And the distinguishing feature of church law and church governance is that this ruling idea is unique; it is the recognition that Jesus Christ is Lord, the Head of the church, and that the church is his Body (Oostenbrink-Evers, 2000, 282). It is essential for Church order, Church law, that the church is unique in her own nature. She is not an instance of a broader category, but a category to herself.

When we reflect on Church order, we have first of all to ask what the Scripture says. To be sure, there is no one church order to be found in New Testament, because the church in apostolic times had developed very few fixed forms. We do find some basic thoughts in the Bible as to the essence of the church; there should always be some scriptural basis in historical processes of changing church order. Scholten mentions two basic principles.

5.1. Community

The first principle is this: the Church is the gathering of the community of Christ believers. Coming together in the name of Jesus Christ determines its existence. In this 'coming together' there is a link with God and with each other. The being together, listening to the proclamation of God's Word together, participating in the sacraments together, and worshiping together constitutes its essence.

This excludes all domination of a hierarchy of office holders. The Church is "a sacred meeting of true Christ-believers, all expecting their salvation in Jesus Christ" (CB XXVII). The meeting, not the individual, speaks the decisive word.

5.2. Serving

The second principle: any Office in the Church is the Office of him who serves. For Jesus, serving is better than being served (Mark 10, 45). This does not exclude the fact that people can have authority. However, serving is of a different nature than that of secular rulers. It is not tied to individuals, but to the congregation, and it is derived from the Office of Christ.

6. Conclusion

To facilitate the survival of churches and faith communities, we need church law. Paul Scholten has shown this for the Dutch situation. To appreciate this, we need a proper understanding of both law and church. Among other things, Law is the arrangement of relationships between human beings living together; it applies to a community.

The church is both invisible (an article of faith, the Una Sancta) and the manifestation of this Una Sancta. Scholten challenges the view that the church is essentially invisible. In his view, the church is essentially manifested and shaped in the empirical church, in a community of believers.

The shape of the visible church is not arbitrary because it is the manifestation of the Una Sancta. Therefore, it is not enough to have only functional rules. The shape of the church must correspond as much as possible to the essence of the Una Sancta, its essence as Body of Christ with Christ as its Head.

The Bible provides two principles. One of them is certainly the gathering of the community, listening to the Word of God together, participating in the sacraments and in worship. This excludes all dominating hierarchy. The other basic principle is that any office in the church is modeled on the office of Him who came to serve.

My hope is that Scholten's thinking in the area of church and law may be fruitful to missionary initiatives, so that they may develop into sustainable churches or Christian communities.

APPENDIX

A Tool Kit for building up a sustainable community in a missionary situation

Introduction

Suppose you are involved in a Christian missionary initiative. People react to activities and contacts with Christians, the Christian faith is being discussed and a growing community of faith is getting under way. Adults/teens are involved in varying degrees, from showing some interest to actively participating. You even have a team that is providing a certain measure of leadership. But nothing is official, everything is informal and loose. That atmosphere of informality, the organic way of spending time together feels good.

Meetings

There are regular meetings of a faith-sharing character. For instance, there is singing before a meal, the Bible is opened, and a prayer is said. People become believers, which gives rise to new questions such as: are we going to baptize them? Are we going to celebrate communion? And who will perform the baptism, can you just go and do it? Or do we opt for sending new Christians to existing churches. Are we a church? What is a church anyway?

Organize?

You get to a new stage. What next? Should you really start organizing things on purpose? Would it not be a pity to lose much of the spontaneous and informal 'everyone participates' character of the gathering? But on the other hand: if you do nothing, the initiative will lose some momentum and there is a risk that the community might decline or evaporate. Are you longing to see what had grown up become more durable? What do you need for that? Is it complicated?

Tool kit

To help you with these questions we have developed a tool kit. It is a kit to build a sustainable community of faith as a sequel to a missionary initiative. You could see it as a tool to help you. It consists of a number of questions. If you run through the questions it may clear your thinking on why you do or do not want to take the step to organize a number of issues, whether you want to opt for more continuity, and how.

Arrangements

Organizing things has to do with rules or regulations for relationships, activities and commitments. You have to agree about what is done and not done, about rules. Many people do not like rules. But even at this initial stage there will already be rules, although they are probably not written. We will discover whether writing them down will help you to grow towards durability.

Writing down how things are done, how we have arranged it, who does what and what it is that we actually do, who we are – all these things together are called law, church law. I do not hesitate to claim that there will be no stable community without church law.

This tool kit will offer some helps towards establishing essential rules for a durable Christian community of people, for forming a stable community of faith. You can see the rules as a support. They function like a support beside a growing plant to help the plant, or a sturdy construction for a vine so that the clusters of grapes are supported while they grow and ripen, so they will not touch the soil and be spoiled.

We start from a situation that a small community has grown around a missionary initiative. Suppose you want to make the community more durable . . .

Questions

What follows is a number of questions, clustered by subject matter. They touch on matters such as identity, membership and leadership. They can be followed up with more questions. When you read the questions, you may feel that it is rather much and very comprehensive. But remember you need not answer them all. When you have a small plant, you give it a small support and you don't need to build a big construction right away. As the plant grows, you may need bigger supports and wires to lead the shoots. Developing church law is a growth model that can be fitted to the situation.

Answer the following questions:

A. Identity
   1. Who are you as a Christian community?
   2. What name will you choose as a community?
   3. What is the essence of the community? Club, church, Body of Christ?
   4. What is your communal purpose?

B. Denomination: joining or starting over?

Do you wish to be part of an existing denomination or do you want to stay separate and be non-denominational?

   1. If you join an existing denomination, there will usually be a form of church law in place. E.g. if you choose to become a house church within the

Protestant Church of the Netherlands, or a pioneering spot within that Church. Or something else in another Church?

2. For a non-denominational church or community you need new church laws. The following steps may help.

C. Membership
   1. Who can be a member? Often, we find gradations of involvement. Does this have consequences for taking part in activities? For being on the leadership team? Why or why not?
   2. How do you join the community? What significance is attached to baptism?

D. Leadership
   1. Who makes decisions? Is there one leader or is there a team? Or do all members decide? What do we call this team or meeting?
   2. How is the decision made? Half of the votes plus one, or in unity, or a qualified majority such as two-thirds of the meeting in case of important decisions?
   3. How are the leaders chosen? Do you have voting in writing, raising of hands or by questions asked by the present leadership?
   4. Who are to choose the leaders? Everyone who is involved? The more directly involved? Those who have been baptized? Do you organize a church meeting or special meeting?

E. Consolidation
   1. What do you consider important for your Christian community? Formulate this. This is also part of church law, to describe in a few words who you are, what you do and why.
   2. Celebrating; meetings, church services or worship meetings?
   3. Baptism, Communion: what do these things mean, who may lead, who may take part?
   4. Teaching and training: what content/points of faith do you consider centrally important? And why?
   5. How is it passed on and taught?
   6. Pastoral care: how taking care of each other is organized.
   7. Serving: how will you serve each other and those outside your community?
   8. Practical maintenance of the community:
      - Place of meeting, technical facilities
      - Will you employ people professionally? How will you organize that?
      - What legal form do you want to give this?

F. Legal Form
   1. What legal form will you choose for your Christian community? To take part in legal actions such as hiring a venue, paying a salary etc., you need

to be a legal body such as a corporation or foundation. In the Netherlands you can choose to be an association, a foundation, or simply: a church. Dutch Law has an article about churches. They are ruled by their own statutes. This means you can organize things however you prefer, as long as you organize it properly.

G. Ecumenism, contacts with other churches and Christian communities
   1. Is contact with other faith organizations important to you?
   2. How do you see the Body of Christ? Is your community part of that? How? Are other Christian communities part of it? So, what is your relationship to them? Do you wish to work together with them? How?

This tool kit is being tested in a pilot situation of a missionary project by Youth for Christ in Zwolle, the Netherlands.

Abbreviations and bibliography

CB: Confessio Belgica

Balke, Wim, and Hélène Oostenbrink-Evers. 1995. De Commissie voor de Werkorde (1942–1944). Zoetermeer: Boekencentrum.

Herdenkingsnummer ter gelegenheid van de 100ste geboortedag van Paul Scholten van het Weekblad voor Privaatrecht, Notariaat en Registratie, 106(1975) nr. 5314.

Oostenbrink-Evers, Hélène. 2000. Beginselen en achtergronden van de kerkorde van 1951 van de Nederlandse Hervormde Kerk. Zoetermeer: Boekencentrum.

Scholten, Paul. 1949. Verzamelde Geschriften van wijlen Prof. Mr. Paul Scholten, Deel I. Zwolle: Tjeenk Willink.

Sohm, Rudolph. 1892. Kirchenrecht, I: Die geschichtlichen Grundlagen, Leipzig: Duncker & Humblot.

ASSEMBLIES, SACRAMENTS AND THE UNITY OF THE CHURCH

Allan J. Janssen

The unity of the church rests in God's self, not in what we believe about God (Gunning 2014, 585).

In this contribution I intend to deal with the question: how do the broader assemblies – classes/presbyteries and synods – manifest the unity of the church? I will suggest that the church order consider this question from the perspective of the sacraments. We do not ordinarily think of assemblies as sacramental bodies, and for reasons I shall articulate further on. However, to consider the assemblies apart from the sacraments would represent a deficit in our church order – or so I will argue.

Let me begin with an illustration from a recent meeting of the General Synod of my church (the Reformed Church in America). Our synods can be quite contentious (of late the issue has been human sexuality, but that is only the latest issue to surface division within the church). Fully cognizant that our debates could become so heated that delegates might well stop speaking to one another, the president placed an empty chair at the center of the dais. He told the synod to consider the empty chair as Jesus' presence, thereby symbolizing the One in whom we are united. It was well-intentioned, but tone-deaf to a deeper reality, that we had no need for an ersatz symbol of unity when we are, we confess, in fact united in Christ through Word and Sacrament. Would it make a difference in how our assemblies manifest unity if they were more 'sacramental in their gatherings?

My thesis is that the broader assemblies would manifest the unity of the church as they are gathered by Christ in baptism around the one table of the Lord. They would do so in a representative fashion. For, I will maintain, it is in the nature of assemblies that they are not church, strictly speaking, but exist to govern the church.

To pursue the investigation of this claim, I have looked at the church order of four communions that are ordered as presbyterial-synodical: the Christian Reformed Church in North America, the Protestant Church in the Netherlands, the Presbyterian Church (U.S.A.) and the Reformed Church in America.

Assumptions

I make the following assumptions in furthering my argument:

1. Christ gathers the church through Christ's presence in Word and Sacrament. Thomas Torrance put it: "... it is as the Word becomes event in the sacramental ordinances that the Church as body takes shape and form under the ordering of the Word of the ascended Head" (Torrance 1993, 76).

2. The church is ordered around Christi's presence proclaimed from the pulpit and celebrated in the sacrament. Torrance again: "The purpose of this order is to make room in the midst for the presence of the risen Christ so that the Church's fellowship becomes the sphere where the resurrection of Christ is effectively operative here and now" (Torrance, 67). Or as A.A. van Ruler puts it more fetchingly, the order of the church forms the rafters of the cathedral of love; the order creates the space in which the liturgy of the church finds its proper place (cf. Van Ruler 1971, 166).

The church's order performs this task as it determines the time, place and circumstance in which preaching and the sacraments take place. More crucially, it guards the integrity of the sacraments as it oversees who will preside at pulpit and table, thereby manifesting the integrity of the gospel as it echoes the witness of the apostles and prophets. The broader assemblies have as a primary task the manifestation of the apostolic nature of the gathered congregation. As Torrance puts it, "... the Sacraments mean the enactment of the authority of Christ over the Church and its life and ministry and so the ministry of the Word and Sacraments involves a charisma of oversight (episcope) over the whole congregation and its worship, in which the unity of Word and Sacrament, and the proper relation of Sacrament to the Word may be maintained in the Church which is the Body united in Christ as its Head" (Torrance, 77).

3. The church is gathered as a congregation of believers. The church exists as it is embodied. The Heidelberg Catechism puts it that the "Son of God through his Spirit and Word. ... gathers, protects and preserves for himself a community ['Gemeinde', 'congregation'] for eternal life and united in true faith. ... " (HC A54). Or as the Belgic Confession has it: "We believe and confess one single catholic or universal church – a holy congregation and gathering of true Christian believers. ... " (BC, art. 27). The church, then, is not, in the strict sense embodied in the office-bearers of the church. Office-bearers gathered in assembly are a sort of 'skeleton' of the church, one sees the church as in an x-ray photograph (see Van Ruler 1965, 104).

4. The unity and the catholicity of the church exist in Christ. The church's unity is not constituted by means of human agreement in matters of faith. The Presbyterian Church (U.S.A.) says it like this in its Book of Order: "Unity is God's gift to the Church in Jesus Christ. Just as God is one God and Jesus Christ is our one Savior, so the Church is one because it belongs to its one Lord Jesus Christ" (BO F-1.0302).

The presence of Christ

How then do the broader assemblies manifest unity? While the assemblies gather to govern the church, they come together as a body that worships. The church order of my own church, the Reformed Church in America, prescribes that the classis shall begin and end its sessions with prayer and that a sermon may be preached (BCO 1.II.4.1). The General Synod is required to celebrate the Sacrament of the Lord's Supper during each session of the synod (BCO 1.IV.4.4). Similar prescriptions exist for the Presbyterian Church (U.S.A.) for meetings of all its greater assemblies (councils) (BO G-3.0301, G-3.0401, G.3.0501).

The foundational unity of the church, then, is enacted not as the body gathers to do its business, but is established by God in Christ's presence in the midst of the assembly. Pieter Coertzen states that "[i]in every church meeting, in every gathering of church members, people must be prepared to follow the path of the Word" (Coertzen 1998, 22). As I noted at the outset, assemblies have been known to provide ersatz symbols of unity. Some years ago, an initiative called 'Worshipful Work' attempted to infuse the dry and often contentious meetings of church bodies with a sense that they functioned in the presence of God. A laudable notion. A consistory meeting might begin with the lighting of a candle to symbolize the presence of Christ – or of the Spirit. That seems rather impoverished when the church already has Christ as present in Word (Coertzen's point) and sacrament.

If this is the case – if the unity of the church has already been established in Christ and, moreover, that that unity has been enacted in the assembly in the presence of Word and Sacrament – then the unity of the church manifest in the broader assembly is not a function of the agreement or disagreement on matters that are before the assembly. Differences will persist, deep differences. Officebearers may sense that unity with those who differ is difficult. In fact, from our all-too-human perspective, it may be impossible. But the differences are not decisive. In fact, our human divisions, including especially those rooted in our sinful actions, have already been overcome in Christ.

The local congregation

From a Presbyterian-Reformed perspective, there are, however, problems with envisioning the sacraments at the core of the work of the broader assemblies. Fundamental to the four church orders under examination in this paper is the fact that the celebration of the sacraments is located in the local congregation. It is the task of the session, or the consistory, or the board of elders, to oversee the celebration of the sacraments. The church order (Constitution) of the Protestant Church of the Netherlands is exemplary: "The Lord's Supper is celebrated under the responsibility of the church council with due respect for the guidelines laid down by the church" (KO, art. IX.4). Moreover, in their *ordinanties*, it states that the "Lord's Supper is celebrated in a church service of a congregation" (ord. 7–3-2) or in irregular circumstances "the Lord's Supper can be administered under the authority of a church council in a church service in institutions like prisons, hospitals and orphanages" (ord. 7–3-4). The celebration of the sacraments (here specifically the Supper) takes place within the local congregation under the direction of the local assembly.

There is a suggestion of an older practice when the Christian Reformed Church requires that a church designated by a synod convene the following synod (CO, Art. 14). In this way, the celebration of the Lord's Supper at the synod takes place under the auspices of a local church council. At one time, this had been the practice in the Reformed Church in America. The celebration of the Supper was then administered under the authority of a local board of elders. Thus the synod, in effect, gathered with the local congregation at the place where the sacrament constitutes the community, the *Gemeinde*.

The prescription that the sacrament be administered under the authority of the local assembly is rooted both in the nature of the church and the nature of the broader assemblies. As our initial assumptions have made clear, the church is gathered around Word and Sacrament and is so as a gathering of believers (the baptized). In principle, it is the church as a whole that gathers, the church catholic. It is not only office-bearers who gather at the table, but office-bearers together with all the people of God are gathered by Christ at the one table. No class of persons is excluded. It is the case, of course, that a celebration of the Supper at a meeting of a broader assembly does not exclude; believers who are present are invited to the table. Nonetheless, when the body gathers as assembly, it excludes by the very constitution of its membership.

The assemblies then, are not fully catholic. Hence, the assemblies are not church except in a representative sense (as a gestalt). In a Reformed understanding, those who gather around the table are united in Christ, and so united with each other. All communions would agree to that claim. The Reformed take another step: as united with each other, they are responsible to one another for their life in Christ's community. That co-responsibility is expressed as members in Christ (and so of the church; membership in the church is membership at the Table) in being under the discipline of a board of elders. Hence, the broader assemblies are not, and cannot be, the church in the same sense that the local congregation is the church.

Confession as agreement?

That is not to say that the assemblies do not have an essential role to play in the life of the church. As the Presbyterian Church puts it, the "councils of the church exist to help congregations and the church as a whole to be more faithful participants in the mission of Christ". They do so as, among other things, they "provide that the Word of God may be truly preached and heard ... " and "provide that the Sacraments may be rightly administered and received" (BO G-3.0101, G-3.0201). The greater assemblies 'assist'. They do so as they educate and ordain ministers of Word and Sacrament, as they oversee the life and work of ministers, as they oversee the actions of boards of elders, as they function as courts of the church, as they work with the confessions of the church. In short, the broader assemblies exist for the governance of the church. As our initial assumptions have put it, they are ordered around Word and Sacrament, but their primary connection is not direct.

And yet, as the church orders have prescribed (and as it happens in practice), the broader assemblies do celebrate the Lord's Supper. And yet they are not shaped sacramentally. They are not a local congregation. As I have been claiming, they exist primarily to be about the governance of the church. It is not surprising, then, given the parliamentary shape of our broader assemblies that we think that unity is to be found in agreement in doctrine (or, of late, in moral conviction). Is it possible to view the sacrament as a means of manifesting the unity of the church? We can, I think, if we consider how the broader assemblies gather. And that step is to reflect for a moment on confession.

It may appear that we have fallen back into the problem of conceiving unity as a matter of agreement. We agree on a confession; we have voted on it, after all. We come together because we share a common commitment to the truth of the gospel, the truth articulated in a common confession. And that, of course, has been a sticking point among the church, including especially those of a Reformed/Presbyterian stripe. We do not agree on confessional matters; hence we divide, and do so as a matter of principle.

But that, I think, is to misunderstand the nature of confession. Confession is not an attempt to come to unity by virtue of agreement. Or so I argue. We can, of course, find historical examples of attempts to forge unity by virtue of discovering a common confession. I argue, in contradistinction, that confession is an acknowledgement of a truth that exists. Or to put it more clearly, confession stands as witness to the truth. As the Presbyterian Church has it, "[i]n its confessions, the Presbyterian Church (U.S.A.) witnesses to the faith of the Church catholic" (BO, F-2.03). I would put it a bit differently and say that the confessions witness to the One in whom we believe.

The assemblies manifest unity around the confessions in an indirect way. The Acta of the Synod of Emden, the first church order of the Dutch Reformed Church, requires ministers to have signed on to the Belgic Confession, or in the case of the French churches, the Gallican Confession (KH, 72). Even today, ministers in the Reformed Church in America, e.g., are required to subscribe to a ministerial declaration that states that the confessions are "historic and faithful witnesses to the Word of God" (BCO, Formulary #3). This is not the case for elders although, again in the Reformed Church in America, upon ordination an elder promises to "accept the church's order and governance, submitting to ecclesiastical discipline" should she or he "become delinquent in either life or doctrine" (WTL, 47). There is, however, no mention of the church's confessions except indirectly (the 'Standards' being stated in the preamble to the church order). In this way, the assembly is a gathering of those who acknowledge faith in the particular God as witnessed, i.e. confessed, by the church.

Baptism

Still, we may have recourse to a deeper reality, one that is founded on the baptismal confession. Office-bearers come as the baptized, and so as those who have been engrafted into Christ. This is not conceived apart from confession. The ritual of baptism includes the ancient baptismal confession, the so-called 'Apostles' Creed'.

Through baptism and confession, then, the broader assemblies acknowledge, give articulation to, their faith in the One who is Lord and Savior, whose reign has begun, and in whose future we live and move and have our being. They do so as representative of the church. That is the broader assemblies are the church in torso. They are a gestalt of the church. They are not the church in its fullness, but represent the church. And they acknowledge their unity as they gather. They do so as a gestalt of the church that manifests faith, a faith that is the humble acknowledgement of the One who gave himself for the sake of the world.

As the baptized are now gathered at Table, this liturgical reality in turn shapes the life of the community, here the assembly. The work of James K.A. Smith helps us here. In *Imagining the Kingdom*, he describes the nature of liturgy. His larger project is to examine what he calls 'cultural liturgies', practices that follow particular patterns. Those patterns in turn shape not only our behavior but also our beliefs. Smith is tilting against the notion that it is our 'worldview', our mental take on reality that in turn shapes behavior. Rather liturgies shape habits and shape them at our deepest selves. While Reformed Christians have not been 'non-liturgical' in their collective life (indeed, according to Smith we may be engaged in liturgical practices in ways other than the Sunday morning service of worship), the liturgies of our common worship have been attenuated at best, often limited to services of the Word. What would happen if our assemblies became more sacramental in nature? Would it make a difference if the Lord's Supper were celebrated at every session of the assembly? Would it make a difference if concrete symbols of baptism were present and enacted in such a way that the officers would enact the fact that their offices were rooted in baptism? Would the practice of the sacraments shape how the assembly functions as it deliberates on difficult issues?

Humble bodies

Put another way: the 'table' around which the assembly gathers is no ordinary table. It is not the table in a board room. The table has been sanctified. It is the Lord's table, for this is the Lord's church.

The representative body that gathers as a torso of the fullness of the body of Christ, will gather as servant. Its unity being constituted in the Christ present in the Supper results in the assemblies being gathered as humble bodies. Torrance reminds us that the "form of priesthood in the church derives from the Form of Christ as the Form of the Suffering Servant" (Torrance 1993, 82). He goes on to say that "what the Church does at the Table in communion with the Body of Christ broken for the world and in communion with the Blood of Christ shed in propitiation for the sins of the whole world, the Church is commanded to act out its life and ministry, and if need be, to be broken in its own body and to shed its own blood for Christ's sake and the Gospel's" (Torrance, 86). Would the assembly then not stand humbly before its Lord and before all the world as servant? Would the sacraments shape the broader assemblies as servant, not just to the functioning of the church, but in humble service to its Lord and to the Lord's reign?

This, then, is the people of God, the body of Christ, the community of the Holy Spirit gathered prayerfully to deliberate not about how to promote its own set of beliefs, not to 'promote' anything at all, but how God desires to use this fragile institution for God's own purposes. Here, after all, is the church, now gathered around Word and Sacrament, which is to say, gathered by the Crucified Messiah who is Lord!

Abbreviations and bibliography

BC: Belgic Confession.
BCO: Book of Church Order, Reformed Church in America.
BO: Book of Order, Presbyterian Church (U.S.A.).
CO: Church Order and Its Supplements, Christian Reformed Church in North America.
HC: Heidelberg Catechism.
KH: *Kerkelijk Handboekje* 1882. Kampen: Zalsman.
KO: Kerkorde en ordinanties van de Protestantse Kerk in Nederland.
WTL: Worship the Lord, Reformed Church in America.

Coertzen, Pieter. 1998. Church and Order: A Reformed perspective. Leuven: Peeters.
Gunning Jr., Johannes H. 2014. Verzameld werk 2. Zoetermeer: Boekencentrum.
Smith, James K.A. 2013. Imagining the Kingdom: how Worship Works. Grand Rapids: Baker Academic.
Torrance, Thomas F. 1993. Royal Priesthood: A Theology of Ordained Ministry. Edinburgh: T&T Clark.
Van Ruler, Anton A. 1965. Reformatorische opmerkingen in de ontmoeting met Rome. Hilversum: Paul Brand.
Van Ruler, Anton A. 1971. Theologisch werk II. Nijkerk: Callenbach.

A SEARCH FOR ECCLESIASTICAL UNITY IN EARLY MODERN FRENCH PROTESTANTISM

Herman Speelman

Introduction: Where is the unity of the Church to be sought?

French Protestants, by proclaiming themselves a separate church denomination in 1559, expressly defied government policy. At the same time, they set course for asking that same government to recognize them as an independent ecclesial body within French society alongside the Roman Catholic Church. Until that time, it had been almost unthinkable that several different ecclesial bodies could coexist at the same time in one area. By taking this revolutionary step, they challenged the unity of church and state while breaking ecclesiastical unity. At the same time, they attempted to achieve a close unity within their own church denomination by maintaining a strict mutual spiritual and social discipline. Internally they sought strength more in an ecclesiastical structure than in the holy sacrament as the unifying body of Christ.

From the very beginning of the Reformation in France up to the colloquy of Poissy, however, the significance of the Eucharist was a key theme. In the age of the Reformation, the sacrament of the altar often functioned as a 'fission fungus' instead of social cement or a unifying element in the ecclesiastical community. Both Catholics and Protestants used the well-known metaphor of the body of Christ (*corpus Christi*) to refer to both the church and the Eucharist as an expression of the unity of the ecclesiastical society and of the church. When the biblical notions of *communion* and *corpus* (e.g., 1 Cor. 11 and 12) were used as ecclesiological concepts (for example in the late medieval period) they retained their sacramental force. Expressions such as *corpus Christi* and *communio sanctorum* never completely lost their sacramental connotations in ecclesiology (cf. Elwood 1999). In our time the familiar images of the Christian church as the body of Christ and as a communion of believers are widely accepted conceptual models.

Due to a shift in church polity in France in the beginning of the 1560s, some substantial changes occurred with great influence in the other parts of the world. 1562 is the year in which religious plurality first took shape in the Western world (cf. Speelman 2014, 200–207). However, after the defeat of the reformed Confederates in the Battle of Kappel of 1531, Appenzell and St. Gallen/ Toggenburg had already remained territories with two confessions equal in status and with equal rights (Bryner 2016, 250, 253 and 262). In the same year Jean Morély, Sire de Villiers, an active Calvinist layman, defended a less clerical church structure, one established apart from the French Reformed ecclesiastical structures of 1559, in his *Traicté de la discipline et police chrestienne* (Morély 1562). Amidst disagreement and conflict within Protestant ranks, in 1565 the fifth national synod of the French Reformed churches requested the Protestant minister Antoine de la Roche, Baron of Chandieu, to defend the official Reformed church polity. His *La confirmation de la discipline ecclesiastique* appeared a few months later (Chandieu 1566, see also: Speelman 2017).

In an attempt to strengthen their position, the French Calvinists strove to organize themselves into one efficiently functioning synodical church structure with a tiered delegation of representatives of regional assemblies and through them, of the church members. There was also an emphasis on their independence of the state, seeking a status that would (on this point) be comparable with the status of the Roman Catholic Church. Morély and his followers had in mind a church order in which the ordinary church member (which meant the wise male church members who had no specific ecclesiastical office) could have the final say, even in decisions regarding doctrine and life.

What were the effects of the French Calvinists' search in the sixties for more ecclesiastical unity on (1) a new church leadership, (2) the development of religious plurality, and (3) discipline or church polity?

1. From assemblies of believers to a clerical institution (at the end of the 1550s)

1.1. Church as a communion of believers

When referring to the process of church formation in France, with people gathering spontaneously as they had done in the 1540s, and with a more formal church structure emerging in the late 1550s, the status of these groups, worshipping by reading the Bible, praying and singing together in secret meetings, can best be captured, as Sara Barker rightly suggested, by the term *assemblée des fidèles* (see Barker 2009, 57).

When Antoine de la Roche-Chandieu, minister of the Reformed church in Paris, stayed in Poitiers in the autumn of the year 1558, he was commissioned (possibly by the provincial synod of Poitou) to examine the possibility of convoking a first national synod of the French Reformed Church. It was a year after the brutal disruption of an illegal assembly held in the rue Saint Jacques on the evening of 4 September 1557. Towards the end of this meeting, shortly after the Lord's Supper had been celebrated, hundreds of participants, men and women, had been crudely attacked, captured and even killed in a raid led by monks and students. It was deeply felt that this action could not remain without response, but what the appropriate response should be, was under discussion among the churches.

After years of persecution, the continuously harassed fugitive believers had grown accustomed to their clandestine life in small underground churches and they considered themselves principally *communions des fidèles.* Hundreds of smaller and larger of such churches had arisen throughout the country, bringing together millions of supporters and members. In the 1560s, a new generation of Reformed church leaders, like Chandieu and Beza, took up the baton in France, building upon the innovative thoughts of the previous generation and trying to transform the Reformed ideas of church polity – especially those of Geneva – to a national level in the Kingdom of France and to consolidate these for the future, in an attempt to establish a Reformed orthodoxy.

While the Protestant believers were scattered all over the country and had difficulty convening, they experienced being a member of a local church as belonging to the invisible spiritual body of Christ (*corpus Christi*), the sacral communion of saints, 'citizens united in a community or a congregation', 'the multitude and assembly of men chosen by God's grace', and 'united as citizens of one community (or city-state)'. With regard to 'church', Théodore de Bèze confessed that the church consists of 'all believers', spread out among many places, but united and connected with each other like citizens of a city-state (*communauté*), in so far as all partake in the privileges of Jesus Christ. This participation in the privileges of Christ, Beza went on to say, we call that the 'communion of saints' (*communauté des saincts*). And thereby Beza zooms in on the individual believer (cf. De Bèze 1557, ad Mt 16:18, fol. 26; cf. De Bèze 1560, De Bèze 1561, art. 5.4 and 5.8; cf. De Brès 1561,CB, art, 27 and 29). John Calvin also very much underlined the difference between the sacral community (*corpus Christi*) from the civic commune (*corpus politicum*) (CO 49, at 1 Cor. 12:12, 501).

In 1559, the French Confession described 'church' in a similar way, as 'the company of the faithful' (*compagnie des fidèles*) (CG, art. 27; cf. CB, art. 27: 'the assembly of true Christian believers'). In the Protestant way of thinking, one was no longer a Christian solely because of birth or infant baptism, but being a Christian had become a matter of conscious choice. No longer was the institution of the church to control life through its system of sacraments, but believers themselves were to make free use of the instruments of grace offered to them by the Gospel. The churches in France were to become "a uniformly godly community" through "disciplining of people's daily lives", Karen Spierling concludes (Spierling 2008, 100). The church members became personally responsible for seeking and maintaining the union of the church by submitting "to the public teaching, and to the yoke of Jesus Christ", so the French protestant church confessed in 1559 (CG, art. 26). From the start of Protestantism the churches in Germany and in the Swiss Cantons were supported by the government and often also openly by charismatic preachers. In France there was at first an active persecution policy so that it was not without danger for evangelical believers to openly come out for their faith.

If they were to live out this understanding of the church the French Reformed (i.e., the Huguenots) saw no other way than to enter into a mild, diplomatic, yet 'radical', confrontation with the government. The preparations were made in the greatest secrecy, since the plan for a synod amounted to a conscious transgression of the government policy and would elicit a sharp response were it to become known. It soon did come into the open that the Huguenots were intent on establishing an ecclesiastical organization of their own, a national synodical alliance, without the approval of the state. The decision taken by the first national synod of Paris in late May 1559 to establish a national confession without approval from the state formed a turning point. A question immediately followed: to what extent should this new church structure be more or less aristocratic or democratic? The debate on this question revealed two conflicting views on the church.

1.2. The desire for lay participation in decision-making

With his *Traicté de la discipline et police chrestienne*, Morély became in 1562 the leader of the first formidable internal attack on the structure of the French Reformed Church. He did not come from the highest ranks of nobility, but was from a family accustomed to serving at the royal courts and belonged to that group of noble converts who made Calvinism into a potent force in sixteenth-century European politics. Both his father and his father-in-law had apparently served the court of Francis I, King of France, as physicians and Morély himself was to serve the court of Jeanne d'Albret, Queen of Navarre, as a tutor. He became a Protestant somewhere around 1547, and moved to Geneva somewhere in the 1550s, when many other French Protestants were crowding into that city. Twice Morély got into trouble with the city's leading pastors (cf. Denis and Rott 1993, Kingdon 1967, 44f.).

While Morély endured a relatively negative image for quite a period of time, in the previous century Henri Naef reasserted his importance by describing him as one of the first defenders of 'equality and Christian freedom', and a short while later Emile Léonard described him as a Congregationalist, the victor of "Congregationalism in the French Reformation", the movement which had emerged from "meetings relating to the Bible" (cf. Denis and Rott 1993, 104, n. 43. Léonard 1961, 115ff.).

Morély wished to reinstate the churches' freedom and independence, and it was his opinion that the churchgoers should have discretion over church affairs such as doctrine, excommunication, the election of the preachers, and vigilant defense of unity across the churches (cf. Morély 1562, 75). His more democratically inspired church structure design, however, did not coincide with the more clerical presbyteral-synodical plan outlined in the *Discipline des Eglises réformées de France* in 1559. As a result, the unity of this young and unprecedented French Protestant church was at stake.

In Morély's opinion, the church should not be governed from the top down, but from the bottom up. This guarantees the unity in the church. He advocated people living and deciding together, according to the order of Christ, without a specific chair or city, person or church exerting supremacy over the others. Such claims to supremacy were also prohibited in the more hierarchically designed presbyteral-synodical church structure of the Reformed church, one principle being utterly clear in the synod's formulation of the first French church order – in John Quick's later English version of the*Discipline des Eglises réformées de France*: "No Church, nor Church-Officer, be he Minister, Elder, or Deacon, shall Claim or Exercise any Jurisdiction, or Authority over another" (Quick 1692, vol. 1, p. 2, ch. 2; cf. Benedict and Fornerod 2012, 1–7; cf. Niesel 1939, 73; cf. Mentzer and Van Ruymbeke 2016, 20). But this principle was not consistently applied in the end nor applied to the office-less church member. The representatives of certain churches took decisions for others without consulting them. It is primarily this idea of representation that Morély denies (cf. Morély 1562, 70, 81, 294) and Chandieu defends (cf. Chandieu 1566, 121, 127, 143, 180–191; cf. Denis and Rott 1993, 171f and 205f; cf. Speelman 2017, 58–65).

This was unacceptable for Morély. Church councils and other gatherings only have an advisory function, he claimed, and "no power at all to determine or decide anything" (Morély 1562, 289) that should be decided over by a local church on the basis of consensus. This was a basic principle for him. Just as Morély sanctified his 'democratic' church structure, a person like Beza did the same with his aristocratic model, in which Christ is not represented by the gathering of believers, but by the consistory (cf. Maruyama 1978, 117, 121v). The position of the church council is somewhat different in the vision of Bucer and Viret, as it only has an administrative function. They distinguish between the judicial and administrative power of the church, or, in other words, between those who have the 'power' and those who execute 'functions'. They placed the actual power in the hands of the gathering believers (cf. Denis and Rott 1993, 150).

2. Ecclesiastical unity via plurality (in the beginning of the 1560s)

2.1. The unity of the Church and the unity of the nation

Many who lived in the 16th century were in fact late medieval people, from a world of order and unity, a world also full of old traditions and superstitions. But in that society, church life was rapidly changing. People like Morély and Chandieu sought to introduce some order into that new world, and also into the great Kingdom of France, so heartily loved by all. But the concept of a gathered church of true Christians as the secret and spiritual body of Christ and as visible sacral community within that same Kingdom, without the cooperation of the civil governments, ran counter to the ideal of civic unity and of the unity of the visible church (cf. Oberman 2009, 188; Speelman 2014, ch. 3.2.). The price paid for this limited degree of freedom, however, was the demise of the religious unity of church and state.

2.2. The moderate view of the party of the Huguenots and of the Moyenneurs

The Huguenots closed their ranks, determined as they were no longer to be treated as heretics. In the early 1560s, the French Protestants were hopeful about the future in the shifting political situation. The policy of persistent persecution by the court of Henry II and the House of De Guise had come to an end, and, under the directions of queen mother Catherine de Médicis, statesman Michel de L'Hôpital and the *moyenneurs*, the climate had become considerably more tolerant. In the end, the monarchy deviated from its prior course by renouncing the religious unity of the realm.

At the French court the question regarding a policy of reconciliation gradually grew in importance. The former policy of persecution had passed, and under the leadership of the new Chancellor, Michel de l'Hôpital, a new policy was introduced. L'Hôpital soon showed himself to be the leading spokesman at the court for the *moyenneur* party. Like the Huguenots, the more moderate or '*moyenneurs*' were ready to meet with the different parties; both *moyenneurs* and Huguenots favored a peaceful solution to the conflict. Contrary to the Huguenots, however, the *moyenneurs* were intent on keeping the different groups within the one established church, at all costs. At the meeting of the Estates General in Orléans in December 1560, Chancellor Michel de l'Hôpital presented himself as one of the leading spokesmen of the *moyenneur* party.

At that time, it was simply unthinkable to L'Hôpital for two opposing ecclesiastical orders to be able to live together in peace. He is well known for his remark that a Frenchman and an Englishman with the same religion can understand each other better than two citizens of the same city of a different confession.

This statement was not motivated merely by the close ties between French and English Protestants. His statement also confirmed the commonly held view that a kingdom ought to be united in religion. But France was in these days not a true political unity. France was, after all, partly in British hands, and further included a number of more or less independent kingdoms and noble families, like the De Bourbons in the West, Montmorency in the Center (to whom De Coligny also belonged), and the De Guises in the East. The maintenance of religious unity was thus regarded as of prime importance in order to preserve the unity of the French nation as a whole. Otherwise France would be the first kingdom or empire, whether small or large, that had two officially recognized churches. In the great German empire, comprising many small states, every prince had, since the Peace of Augsburg (1555), been free to choose between Roman Catholicism and Lutheranism. But the ruler did have to make a choice between the two.

L'Hôpital's statement at the assembly of the Estates General in Orléans, in which he highlighted the importance of religious unity for the entire kingdom, is to be understood against this background. The French government did not want the kingdom to crumble along the lines of religious confession as had happened in the German empire.

The queen mother, Catherine de Medici, as well as the chancellor, l'Hôpital, together with many others of the *moyenneur*-party, were open to the proposals of the Huguenots. The *moyenneurs* and the French Calvinists were both interested in seeking a solution to the growing religious controversies in France through dialogue. L'Hôpital did not look upon the Reformed as heretics, "since the entire difference is that they want to reform the church in the spirit of the early church" (*"tout leur différend est en cela qu'ils veulent que l'eglise soit réformée en la façon de la primitive"*; Buisson 1950, 189). However, while the *moyenneurs* wanted to bring the differing religious currents together so that they could continue to function within a single ecclesiastical structure, the Huguenots no longer considered this a feasible option. Concretely, this meant that they sought some form of recognition on the part of the government, that is, a modest place in society alongside the large state church.

2.3. The colloquy in Poissy, the last attempt to preserve unity

The long-awaited religious dialogue, in which the Eucharist was a key theme, took place in the Dominican priory at Poissy in the fall of 1561. Theologically, the colloquy of Poissy was a failure, and it is entirely possible that conservative Roman Catholics consciously aimed to effect such a failure. All the same, Poissy was not without effect for the Calvinists.

This national assembly in Poissy represented a final attempt on the part of the political leaders and representatives of the established church, together with the

Calvinists, to seek a common solution to the existing religious conflicts and, if at all possible, to maintain the unity of the French nation. To that end, the government invited the opposing parties to seek a way to restore unity within the church "in order to reunite them to the church of Rome" (*"de les reunir à l'Eglise Romaine";* Baum a.o. 1883, 521), and Antoine de Bourbon, the King of Navarre, who was well-disposed towards the Protestants, spoke in a letter just before the colloquy of "supplying a contribution for the formulation of a good agreement" (CO 18, no. 3477 (Letter from 12 August 1561), 606), so that a solution might be found to France's growing religious problems.

The Huguenots felt that a peaceful solution was closer at hand than ever before. The hopes for recognition in the form of an agreement with the government were increasing. Beza expected that "at the very least the justice of our cause" will be recognized (cf. Aubert a.o. 1963, no. 197, 178). With this, the goal harbored by the Huguenots of obtaining a certain recognition from the government, as well as some religious freedom accompanied by a certain form of independence, seemed more than ever within reach. In the fall of 1561, L'Hôpital had made a radical turn in his thinking on religious policy, and now inclined to the position of the party of the influential governor and admiral of France, Gaspard de Coligny, Count of Châtillon and of high noble origin, who during his long imprisonment after the Spanish victory at Saint-Quentin in 1557 had converted to the evangelical faith and had become one of the main leaders of the Huguenots. The road of dialogue had failed. The final outcome of all these discussions was that L'Hôpital came to realize that church unity was no longer possible. The effort to find a single ecclesiastical organization that Roman Catholics and Protestants would freely join had failed. Both at Orléans and at Poissy L'Hôpital had failed to bring the different groups together.

2.4. On the way to religious plurality and national unity

In the wake of the colloquy of Poissy, it had become clear that the efforts of the *moyenneurs* to keep the different religious currents together within a single church had failed. Thus, after Poissy they were ready to seek a solution to the religious conflict that was more in line with the Huguenot proposals. This solution implied that the government would have to recognize the Calvinist church, and that two churches would exist side by side in the kingdom of France. The new edict of Saint-Germain on 17 January 1562, the unique so-called *January edict*, a decree of tolerance, which followed soon after, would be an important step on the way to this religious pluralism.

The unfeasibility of ecclesiastical unity in a single church represented a political reality for L'Hôpital. After Poissy, he therefore opted for a different foundation to his religious policy. It had to be possible "to live in freedom with those who do not observe the same ceremonies as we do" (Doumergue 1927, 272). L'Hôpital made a turn in his thinking within a short span of time by stating that "a person is a Frenchman regardless of his confession" (Nürnberger 1948, 131f.). At the same conference in Saint-Germain, he proposed that the solution to the religious controversies in France was not to be sought "in a religious measure, but in a political one" (Buisson 1950, 196). He did not think in terms of a religious compromise anymore, but of a political compromise. He thus proposed a *modus vivendi*, a realizable agreement that would make it possible for the two churches to dwell alongside one another in peace. This would show itself to be an important first step worldwide on the road to confessional and ecclesiastical plurality.

Calvin had been unable to thwart this inevitable process. After all, he had not been involved in the negotiations that took place with the French court in Saint-Germain. In his view, the most this discussion could achieve was some space within the established church (and Calvin had no interest in that), or a modest place for the Reformed alongside and apart from the existing church (and in Calvin's mind this was simply absurd). In this line, there is no indication whatsoever that he ever approved of the agreement that had been hammered out in January 1562.

2.5. The longing for more unity within the French Reformed Church

The ideal of a state based on religious and ecclesiastical unity was abandoned and the principle 'One King, One Law, One Faith', presented by L'Hôpital in December 1560, became *Un roi, une loi, déux fois* in the January 1562 Edict, a little over a year later. The members of the Reformed church were henceforth allowed to worship under certain conditions. The quickly expanding evangelical movement, which comprised several factions such as Calvinists, Lutherans, Anabaptists, and Nicodemites, sought ecclesiastical and political ways of reinforcing the unity of their particular part of the church.

Paradoxically, the Huguenots strove for unity in mind and deed within their own ranks through strict prescriptions and hard discipline, while advocating for state recognition of their own church denomination, and thus for religious plurality in the one French Kingdom and for the end of the unity between church and state.

It is not necessary here to pay much attention to the view maintained by the hardline Calvinists and the more traditional supporters of the established church. Both were implacably committed to a national religious monopoly. And although, to Calvin's way of thinking, it was simply unthinkable for two churches to exist side by side in one state, the solution desired by the Reformed in France would prove highly influential in large parts of Western Europe.

3. Marks of the unity of the Church: Word, Eucharist, and discipline

The familiar, age-old notion of a European Christendom guided by the church, whose fixed liturgical and sacramental traditions, repeated rituals, and pastoral care structured and disciplined peoples' whole life, as well as the notion of the *corpus christianum* – all of this more or less changed in the Protestant Reformation. And it has come to an end in our times (cf. Gregory 2012, 154).

First the reformers were interested in a renewed Christian lifestyle. From this perspective, one could explain Calvin's efforts in Geneva to use the centuries-old strong connection between the most holy mystery of the Eucharist and ecclesiastical discipline or what he called 'Christian confession', which he saw to be connected in the same way that the foci of an ellipse are inextricably bound together.

But unlike his pupils, for Calvin – as for the Lutherans – the innermost circle of church life and worship centered on the administration of God's word and the sacraments. Other liturgical ceremonies and habits need not be the same in all places. The Lutheran Confession declares that for true unity in the church as a congregation of saints (*congregatio sanctorum*), "it is enough to agree about the teaching of the gospel and the use of the sacraments" (CA, art. 7; cf. Calvin 1559, 4.1.9). For someone like Bucer, the administration of word and sacrament does not suffice. An additional, necessary feature of the church as 'a communion of confessors' was its discipline, so that its members could make progress in their spiritual lives (cf. Bucer 1544, 157ff; Courvoisier 1933, 79; Maruyama 1978, 20ff; Denis and Rott 1993, 145–151; Kim 2014). Bucer's position is similar to that of Pierre Viret and Marty Vermigli (see Speelman 2017, 32).

In the French Calvinistic churches of the 1560s, however, discipline became a more independent third mark of the church and the celebration of the Lord's Supper became, in the first place, "a moment to heal the fissures within the community and confirm solidarity" (Mentzer 2008, esp. 26 and 41f.) as Raymond Mentzer rightly states. In this line, the Holy Supper was more and more, first of all necessary for the believers, because "those who trust Christ, must walk as he walked", as Zwingli once put it (cf. ZW 2, 807, l.23f.). In Zwingli's view of the Supper, the emphasis rests on the ethical consequences for the congregation celebrating the Supper. The subject of the celebration, in Zwingli's view, is the congregation as the body of Christ (cf. Speelman 2016, 296f.). In celebrating Communion, the congregation committed itself time and again to act as a redeemed church community. Compared to Geneva, the church view of the Reformed Church of France had changed somewhat, and discipline became more independent regarding the original meaning of the Holy Supper.

The emphasis was laid more on membership of a congregation and, in this sense participation at the Lord's Table was, in the first place, of community-shaping and unifying significance. The effect was a more horizontal social-ethical, Zwinglian perception of the Holy Communion, whereby the purpose of the Holy Supper became particularly to define the unity and godliness of the Reformed churches. For Calvin, however, the Eucharist was in the first place a mystical, spiritual meal in the Augustinian sense and the church was in the first place a Eucharistic community under a Eucharistic Church Order, although he also emphasized the relationship between the church and the wider society, locally and globally (cf. Speelman 2016, ch. 9 and ch. 11.2 and 3; see also Speelman 2017a, 164f.).

3.1. Membership of the church

The first debate with Morély concerning the most preferable church structure and thus the best route towards ecclesiastical unity within the Reformed Church took place at the third national synod in Orléans in April 1562. This was only a few months after the government gave the Reformed church a modest form of recognition in the January Edict, and only one month after the start of the first religious or civil war in March 1562. The unity of the church was not only threatened by external conflicts; internal issues had to be resolved as well.

The general opinion was that, in order for someone to belong to the church, this person should agree with the French Confession of Faith and should voluntarily submit to the ecclesiastical discipline. Above all, this discipline was a matter of survival and the only way to maintain the unity of the church. The church, in which Christ gathers his own, is the body of Christ, and it is a spiritual body.

According to Morély, the visible church has all the aspects of the church of the chosen, in so far as the order of Christ is functioning. In *De ecclesia* he idealistically writes that the church is the gathering of those "who have been born again and sanctified by the Spirit" ("*Coetus enim hic sanctificatorum erit et regeneratorum*"; Morély 1589, vol. II, 3. See Denis and Rott 1993, 133). The unity of the church, which is central to Morély, is that "of all blessed spirits and souls and the gathering of all believers in Jesus Christ, who for all times are chosen and predestined for eternal life in Jesus Christ, they who precede us as well as they who are to follow us" (Morély 1562, *56*).

For Morély, the administrative board of the church was the 'communion of believers'. Men could take part in this gathering if they had "publicly confessed their faith and were admitted to the communion of the body of the Lord" (Morély 1562, 119f.).

Morély was not a spiritualist. To him, 'church' was not a mere invisible work of the Spirit, along the lines of Gaspard Schwenckfeld or Sebastiaan Franck.

Christ endowed his church with a visible discipline. It is the Spirit that is to transform a person, but this is more than a mere personal affair. Spiritual conversion is also a shared process, taking place in the communion of the church, and the Holy Spirit works through the discipline of the church. Either the church is disciplined, or it isn't, according to Morély, and at the same time the church and its discipline are spiritual. "I know very well", Morély said, "that the church is the spiritual kingdom of Christ [...] and that it is governed by the Spirit. But every one of us partly consists of a spiritual man, in other words, the inner man, reborn by the Spirit of Christ, and partly also consists of an external being that is called to rebirth and justification [...]. However, with regard to the external man that is in us, we also need an external discipline, which Paul calls education [...]. Therefore, we must abide by this order accurately, so that sin within us is controlled. And the same Spirit of Christ, which acts internally with a view to salvation, also acts externally through word and ministry" (in: Denis and Rott 1993, 121f.).

To Morély, discipline was much more than a matter of survival for ecclesiastical life in a hostile environment. The believers' salvation partly depended on it. To achieve salvation, it was important that a person was a member of the church, and to attain this membership a person was to conform to the church order. After all, the church is not merely internal, just as a person is not merely external.

3.2. The position of church members

Morély was not the only one to cherish these innovative church order ideas. Reformers such as Bucer, Vermigli and Viret endowed the church with the characteristics of the *politeia*. They all viewed 'church' primarily as a 'community of believers'. Morély, who adopted this view on church structure and church government, placed himself in an existing tradition (see Denis and Rott 1993, 125–151). It is simultaneously innovative and traditional.

Compared to other reformers, Beza was more innovative – or, should we say, with respect to the Roman Catholic Church, more traditional – in withholding any form of sovereignty from the gathering of churchgoers. In 1559 he still subscribed to the necessity of an "approval of the body of the church" (De Bèze 1559, 162f) during elections. But in the following editions of his *Confession de foy* he revised this view, with the same type of argumentation we saw with Chandieu, "because usually the flock is inexpert and difficult to align and almost always the best part is in the minority" (Beza, art. 35, 210f., and idem, 1561, art. 35, 203f.).

According to Chandieu, the established church finds itself in a state of total destruction. The apostolic order (*discipline Apostolique*) needs to be restored, and this is what happens in the Reformed churches (Chandieu 1566, 39–40). These are 'God's churches' and God recognizes its members 'as members of his universal church'. Its characteristics, i.e., the proclamation of the true doctrine, the pure administration of the sacraments and the use of the ecclesiastical discipline instituted by Christ, are the signs that it is 'God's church', which is also confirmed by the testimonies of its members, more specifically, their "works of mercy", "the perseverance of its martyrs" and the "renewal of their lives" (Chandieu 1566, 16–17).

4. Conclusion

The issues discussed during the development of the French Reformed Church remain issues today, such as, for example the recognition of the Reformed church organization by the state and the reformation of the interdependence of state and church, so that the unity of the state is no longer buttressed by state-enforcement of membership in a single ecclesiastical structure.

From May 1559 on, the Huguenots began more and more to consciously distance themselves from the existing ecclesiastical order in France, and reached a point of no return. The situation was entirely unique. The Anabaptists may indeed have done so as well, but their movement constantly placed them outside of society. The people in France could, as of January 1562, go to different churches without-fear of persecution. A citizen remained a citizen even if he was excommunicated by the church, as L'Hôpital remarked. The way was now open for citizenship to be disconnected from membership in a church.

The new French confession and church order not only stood at the basis of the formation of the Protestant church in France, it also formed a great motive for the European Calvinist movement of other countries to establish independent national churches, as would indeed happen in Scotland, the Netherlands, and Hungary. From then on, the Reformed confessions and disciplines would begin to function worldwide as church-constituting documents.

In the Reformed confessions the most predominant tendency is to define the church as in the late medieval conciliarist tradition as a congregation of the faithful (*communitas fidelium*) (cf. Tierney 1955). In the new era the Protestant leaders in France describe the church less in terms of a company or assembly of believers, but more as an institution. Morély called attention to this shift and proposed an ecclesiastical structure in which the common believer was more in the center of the church. Morély was also headed towards a more mystical understanding of the church, a visible church which, at the same time, transcended the visible. In this regard, he was inspired by the ecclesiastical regulations emerging in the refugee churches. The French Protestant church, however, did not strive for an ecclesiology-of-the-diaspora in this period. Rather the opposite. In fact, the religious and political leaders of the Calvinistic movement in France worked towards a form of public recognition. The great price paid for government recognition of the Reformed church, however, was the demise of religious unity in church and state. The French Protestant church order became also less Eucharistic and the holy meal received a more identity- and community shaping function. The French Calvinists employed the many facets of liturgy and worship to create and sustain religious identity and confessional unity. The Holy Supper received a more community-shaping function. Inclusion in the Eucharist or, conversely, denial of access offered an indication of a person's relationship to fellow believers. Each time the sacral meal was celebrated, every participant had to confirm the value of his membership in a true local church. "Yet it was the Eucharist which defined the Reformed community more than any other liturgical event", Mentzer rightly points out. "The sacrament shaped the very nature of community membership and confirmed a person's position. Most anyone could attend the sermon, but not everyone could take the bread and wine" (cf. Mentzer 2008, 41).

The disagreement between Morély and Chandieu did not concern the church as a communion through Christ in God, but regarded the question whether the church polity should primarily be seen as a clerical institution of church officials, who served the flock, i.e., only their own sheep's, or more as a church of faithful people, a community of 'saints' or an assembly of 'believers'.

In the last century, the expression of church as a *communion of saints* and as the *body of Christ* has received more attention worldwide, not only in the Protestant or evangelical Churches but also in the Roman-Catholic Church. Pius XII invigorated in 1943 the notion of the church as a body, the mystical body of Christ, in the encyclica *Mystici corporis*. In 1964, this notion was reaffirmed in *Lumen gentium*, the ecclesiological centerpiece of the Second Vatican Council, which gave it a sacramental twist. According to the council fathers, Christ, by sending his spirit, "made his brothers ... mystically the components, as it were, of his body" (LG 7, DH 4112). Though this sacramental union with Christ the church is a communion held together by faith, hope and love (LG 8, DH 4118; cf. CTCV, par. 23, 27, 31). Famous and illuminating is also the image that St. Augustine uses in a sermon in which he repeatedly speaks about the 'unity' of the body of Christ and the 'unity' of the church, which he believes resulted from the celebration of the Eucharist: "In this loaf of bread you are given clearly to understand how much you should love unity. I mean, was that loaf made from one grain? ... " (Augustine 1993, 254).

In our times, both these models of church order could probably be beneficial to greater ecclesiastical unity, if they are worldwide, flexible, without a one-sided attention to their own organization, and open, without a tightly bound obligation of membership, without national or group borders. That one and holy universal church, although it might not always be visibly identifiable, should be united in the Triune God through Jesus Christ (see Van der Borght 2010, 293–343).

Abbreviations and bibliography

CA: Confessio Augustana (Augsburg Confession) (1530).
CG: Confessio Gallicana (French Confession) (1559)
CB: Confessio Belgica (Belgic Confession) (1561).
CO: Ioannis Calvini Opera quae supersunt omnia [see Calvin]
CTCV: The Church – Towards a Common Vision. Faith and Order Paper 214. Geneva: WCC 2013.
LG: Lumen Gentium (1965). See: www.vatican.va.
DH: Denzinger – Schönmetzer – Hünermann (eds.). 2012. Enchiridion symbolorum definitionum et declarationum de rebus fidei et morum. 43rd ed. San Francisco: Ignatius Press.
ZW: Huldreich Zwinglis sämtliche Werke [see Zwingli]

Aubert, Hippolyte, Alain Dufour, Henri Meylan et al. (eds.). 1963. Correspondance de Theìodore de Beìze. Vol. 3 (1559–1561). Geneva: Droz.
Augustine, Aurelius. 1993. Sermon 227. In: John E. Rotelle (ed.). 1993. Sermons (184–229Z) on the Liturgical Seasons, vol. III/6 of The Works of Saint Augustine. Trans. Edmund Hill. New Rochelle: New City Press.
Barker, Sarah K. 2009. Protestantism, Poetry and Protest: The Vernacular Writings of Antoine de Chandieu (c. 1534–1591). Cornwall: Ashgate.
Baum, Johann W., August E. Cunitz and Rodolphe E. Reuss (eds.). 1883. [Theodore de Bèze,] Histoire ecclèisiastique des Eìglises Reìformeìes au Royaume de France, vol. 1. Paris: Fischbacher.
Bellitto, Christopher M. (ed.). 2016. A Companion to the Swiss Reformation. Leiden/Boston: Brill.
Benedict, Philip, and Nicolas Fornerod (eds.). 2012. L'organisation et l'action des églises réformées de France (1557–1562). Synodes provinciaux et autre documents. Geneva: Droz.
Beza, Theodorus. 1560. Confessio christianae fidei. Genevae: Iohannis Bonae fidei.
Bryner, Erich. 2016. The Reformation in St. Gallen and Appenzell. In: Bellitto 2016, 238–263.
Buisson, Albert. 1950. Michel de l'Hospital 1503–1573. Paris: Hachette.
Bucer, Martin. 1544. Scripta duo adversaria D. Bartholomaei Latomi L.L. Doctoris et Martini Buceri theologi. Straatsburg: Wendelin Rihel.
Doumergue, Emile. 1927. Jean Calvin: les hommes et les choses de son temps, vol. 7. Lausanne: Bridel.
Calvin, John. 1559. Institutes of the Christian Religion. Two volumes. Edited by John T. McNeill. Translation Ford Lewis Battles 1960. Philadelphia: The Westminster Press – London: SCM.
[Calvin, John]. 1863–1900. Ioannis Calvini Opera quae supersunt omnia. Johann W. Baum, August E. Cunitz, Eduard W.E. Reuss (eds.). 59 vol. Brunsvigae etc.: Schwetschke [CO 1–59 = CR 29–87].
Chandieu, Antoine de la Roche. 1566. La confirmation de la discipline ècclesiastique, observée es églises réformées du royaume de France, avec la response aux obiections proposes alencontre. Geneva: Henri Estienne/La Rochelle: Barthélemy Berton.

Courvoisier, Jaques. 1933. La notion d'Eglise chez Bucer dans son développement historique. Paris: Alcan.
Daussy, Hugues. 2015. Le parti Huguenot: Chronique d'une désillusion (1557–1572). Geneva: Droz.
De Bèze, Théodore. 1557. NT Annotationes I. Genevae: Roberti Stephani.
De Bèze, Théodore. 1559. Confession de la foy chrestienne, contenant la confirmation d'icelle, et la refutation des superstitions contrairers. [Geneva: Conrad Badius]
De Bèze, Théodore. 1561. Confession de la foy chrestienne contenant la confirmation d'icelle, et la refutation des superstitions contraires. Quatrième edition, reveüe sur la Latine, et augmentée avec un Abregé d'icelle, [Caen: Pierre Philippe].
De Brès, Guido. 1561. Confession de Foy, faicte d'un commun accord par les fidèles qui conuersent és pays bas, lesquels desirent viure selon la pureté de l'Euangile de nostre Seigneur Iesus Christ. N.p.
Denis, Philippe, and Jean Rott. 1993. Jean Morély (ca 1524-ca 1594) et l'utopie d'une démocratie dans l'église. Geneva: Droz.
Elwood, Christopher. 1999. The Body Broken: The Calvinist Doctrine of the Eucharist and the Symbolization of Power in Sixteenth-Century France, New York: Oxford University Press.
Gregory, Brad S. 2012. The Unintended Reformation: How a Religious Revolution Secularized Society. Cambridge, Mass.: Harvard University Press.
Halvorson, Michael J., and Karen E. Spierling (eds.). 2008. Defining Community in Early Modern Europe. Cornwall: Ashgate.
Kim, Yosep. 2014. The Identity and the Life of the Church: John Calvin's Ecclesiology in the Perspective of his Anthropology. Cambridge: James Clarke, 156–188.
Kingdon, Robert M. 1967. Geneva and the consolidation of the French Protestant movement, 1564–1572: A Contribution to the History of Congregationalism, Presbyterianism, and Calvinist resistance theory. Geneva: Droz.
Léonard, Emile G. 1961. Histoire générale du protestantisme, vol. II. Paris: Presses Universitaires de France.
Maruyama, Tadataka. 1978. The Ecclesiology of Theodore Beza: The Reform of the True Church. Geneva: Droz.
Mentzer, Raymond A. 2008. Communities of Worship and the Reformed Churches of France. In: Halvorson and Spierling 2008, 25–42.
Mentzer, Raymond A., and Bertrand Van Ruymbeke (eds.). 2016. A Companion to the Huguenots. Leiden/ Boston: Brill.
Morély, Jean. 1562. Traicté de la discipline et police chrestienne. Lyon: Ian de Tournes [Reprinted Geneva: Slatkine 1968].
Morély, Jean. 1589. De ecclesia ab Antichristo per ejus excidium liberanda, aque ex Dei promissis beatissime reparanda Tractatus… London: George Bishop [Reprinted 1594]
Niesel, Wilhelm. 1939. Bekenntisnisschriften und Kirchenordnungen der nach Gottes Wort reformierten Kirche. Zürich: Zollikon.
Nürnberger, Richard. 1948. Die Politisierung des französischen Protestantismus: Calvin und die Anfänge des protestantischen Radikalismus. Tübingen: Mohr (Siebeck).

Oberman, Heiko A. 2009. John Calvin and The Reformation of the Refugees. Geneva: Droz.

Quick, John. 1692. Synodicon in Gallia Reformata: or, The acts, decisions, decrees, and canons of those famous national councils of the Reformed Churches in France, 2 vol. London: T. Parkhurst/J. Robinson.

Speelman, Herman A. 2014. Calvin and the Independence of the Church. Series: Reformed Historical Theology 25. Göttingen: VandenHoeck & Ruprecht.

Speelman, Herman A. 2016. Melanchthon and Calvin on Confession and Communion: Early Modern Protestant Penitential and Eucharistic Piety. Series: Refo500 Academic Studies 14. Göttingen: VandenHoeck & Ruprecht.

[Speelman, Herman]. 2017. Antoine de la Roche Chandieu, De verdediging van het gereformeerde kerkmodel, vertaald en ingeleid door H.A. Speelman. Apeldoorn: Labarum Academic.

Speelman, Herman A. 2017b. At the Lord's Table: Calvin's motives for a frequent celebration of the Holy Supper. In: Pieter H. Vos (ed.), Liturgy and Ethics: New Contributions from Reformed Perspectives. Leiden/ Boston: Brill/ Rodopi, 149–174.

Spierling, Karen E. 2008. The Complexity of Community in Reformation Geneva: The Case of the Lullin Family. In: Halvorson and Spierling 2008, 81–101.

Tierney, Brian. 1955. Foundations of the Conciliar Theory: The Contribution of the Medieval Canonists from Gratian to the Great Schism. Cambridge/Leiden: Brill [reprinted 1998].

Van der Borght, Eduardus. 2010. The Unity of the Church. A Theological State of the Art and Beyond. Leiden/ Boston: Brill.

[Zwingli, Ulrich]. 1905–1929. Huldreich Zwinglis sämtliche Werke. Emil Egli, Georg Finsler (eds.). 14 vols. in 18 Bands. Leipzig: M. Heinsius Nachfolger [Reprinted Zürich: Berichthaus 1959/ Zürich: Theologischer Verlag 1982 [CR 88–101 = ZW 1–14].

MUSYAWARAH UNTUK MUFAKAT EXPRESSING AN ECUMENICAL SPIRIT THROUGH A DECISION-MAKING PROCESS

Roy Alexander Surjanegara

A REFLECTION FROM THE INDONESIAN CONTEXT

A fragile communion and the need for consensus

One of the trickiest issues in the life of the church is decision-making. It could be decisive, but also divisive. There are many close calls, thin lines that separate decisions from divisions, as many who have served in the church long enough could testify. Whether in the congregation councils, in presbytery or synod meetings, in regional or international ecumenical circles, wherever the settings are – we will always have to deal with the issue of coming to a decision. We have witnessed how frail we are as a communion, especially when we became aware how our decision-making methods and approaches are vulnerable to be hijacked by hidden agendas and group interests.

Already in 1978, a Faith and Order Commission meeting in Bangalore considered agreement on decision-making as a visible marker of church unity. The meeting's result was later accepted in the 1983 Vancouver assembly of the WCC, which affirmed three requirements for visible unity:

1. A common understanding of the apostolic faith;
2. Full mutual recognition of baptism, eucharist, and ministry;
3. Agreement on common forms of teaching and decision-making (cf. Gassmann 1994, 14).

Much progress has been made with regard to the first two markers, but there was relatively little with regard to agreement in forms of decision-making, until more than two decades later. In February 2005, the WCC Central Committee meeting finally adopted the consensus model of decision-making after learning the method from the Uniting Church of Australia (UCA) (see Tabart 2003). This adoption signifies the attitude and opinion of the WCC that a decision-making method is not merely a technical or practical matter. It was a gesture that affirmed how the church's decision-making process should also express and reflect its identity (and unity).

The change was made as a result of the work of a Special Commission of Orthodox Participation in the WCC. The Orthodox churches were concerned because they felt that "the present structure of the WCC makes meaningful Orthodox participation increasingly difficult and even for some impossible" (WCC-COP, par. 1). The result of the Special Commission work was fully documented in the Final Report of the Special Commission on Orthodox Participation in the WCC, and one of the main recommendations was to change the WCC's method of decision-making to the consensus model of decision-making (cf. WCC-COP, par. 47). Some important reasons for this change were:

- The existing procedures for decision-making in the WCC were a reflection of the procedures for decision-making in church councils and secular bodies in the continents of the majority of the member churches when the WCC was founded (i.e. in Europe and North America).
- Along with the changing composition of the member churches of the WCC, these procedures do not resonate anymore with some churches – nor with the cultures from which they come from.
- The adversarial nature of the existing procedures where proposals are debated 'for and against' rather then to be explored. Rather than striving to succeed in debate, our aim should be a mutual submission, seeking to "understand what the will of the Lord is" (Eph. 5: 17). In some cultures, [e.g. Indonesia, RAS] this adversarial approach, which can even be confrontational, is something to be avoided.
- The method of voting that was employed had created 'minorities' that had always been outvoted.
- The rigidity of meeting procedures, with the system of motions, amendments, further amendments, points of order and so on, often seemed inappropriate to the complex questions of true Christian obedience, of proper ecumenical relations, and of a Christian approach to historical, social and global change. Procedures that allow more room for consultation, exploration, questioning and prayerful reflection would be likely to promote the purposes of the WCC better than the formal and often rigid procedures that were used. This is not to say that the WCC should attempt to do without rules: on the contrary, rules that are fair, readily understood and workable are essential. The question is the style, content and application of such rules.

- The consensus model provides a set of procedures which makes the best possible use of the abilities, the history, the experience, the commitment and the spiritual tradition of all the member churches.
- The ecumenical movement should accommodate change and development as the issues and circumstances change. To do this means to be open to various expressions of faith and life while remaining true to the "faith that was once for all entrusted to the saints" (Jude 3). The experience of all traditions represented in the WCC is valuable and should be utilized, as and where practical, in the common life, the functioning and the programmes of the Council (cf. WCC-COP, Appendix B, par. 1–7).

The consensus method

So what is the consensus method? The Special Commission gives a description as follows (cf. WCC-COP, Appendix B, par. 8–14): the consensus method is a means of arriving at decisions without voting. It is more conciliar than parliamentary, and more inclusive than adversarial. A consensus is reached, then, when any *one* of the following occurs:

1. All are in agreement (unanimity);
2. most are in agreement and those who disagree are content that the discussion has been both full and fair and that the proposal expresses the general 'mind of the meeting'; the minority therefore gives consent;
3. the meeting acknowledges that there are various opinions, and it is agreed that these be recorded in the body of the proposal (not just in the minutes);
4. it is agreed that the matter be postponed;
5. it is agreed that no decision can be reached.

To use the consensus model would mean not only a change of rule or a technical matter, but more a change of attitude toward coming to a decision. Jill Tabart puts it like this: "Consensus is not intended to mean compromise, but an informed and genuine working through with integrity and vigor to discover a way forward on which all can agree, taking all points of view into consideration" (Tabart 2003, 38). According to her, the means by which churches search for a common mind is as important as the decisions they reach (cf. Tabart 2003, 56f.). That is where the critics toward some disadvantages in the consensus model have been wrong, because they are looking for technical flaws in a system created for spiritual advantages. Compare this with the comment of Joseph Small regarding the democratic captivity of most mainline Protestant denominations in America, where democratic procedures within the churches have developed "in concert with American political and legal culture so that they now play out the least attractive and most unhelpful features of legislative partition, partisan politics, litigious interaction, and perpetual discord" (Small 2014, 62) and seemed to lure many churches decision-making process to simply look for a victory cry from the momentary majority. Leo Koffeman made the following observation, although he was speaking about a different topic here, but the message is nevertheless relevant to appreciate the positive move toward this consensus spirit: "In my view, 'culture' will tend to make up for 'structure' in any ecclesiastical system. A very hierarchical system with a wide range of possible sanctions nearly automatically encourages a culture of disobedience. But the opposite is also true: a system (. . .) which has very limited possibilities to force people and congregations into the desirable attitudes and actions, incites a culture of responsible reception of the 'common good'" (Koffeman 2001, 81). In other words, the technical gap that is perhaps still there in the 'structure' of the consensus model should not be seen as a disadvantage. Rather, it provides space for a 'culture' of responsible reception from the parties involved in the decision-making process.

It is not the intention of this paper to evaluate the effectivity of the consensus model, as it requires further analysis. Rather, it is an affirmation of this positive progress in understanding a decision-making process not just as a method, but as an expression of our unity. Because what is a method, if not an attempt to express what we truly value? Hence if we truly value our unity as a church, it should certainly be visible in how we come to decisions together.

Introducing Indonesia: an example of unity in diversity

As an archipelagic entity that comprises more than 17.000 islands, three different time zones, and a wealth of cultural heritage, Indonesia's diversity is certain. As Frank L. Cooley observes: "Indonesia is made up of many diverse ethnic and language groups, which have been relatively isolated from one another until quite recently. This isolation resulted from the country's marked geographic traits: deep straits and wide seas separating island, high volcanic mountain ranges, heavy tropical rain forests and wide swampy seacoasts. These have led to differences in history, regional development, traditions, customs and religion, which accentuate the difficulty of binding these diverse groups into a unified nation. Indonesia's present condition and her main problem are symbolized by the national motto: *Bhinneka Tunggal Ika*, (Diversity Becoming Unity)" (Cooley 1968, 11).

So, Indonesia cannot be characterized by its wealth of differences nor its challenging geographical features only. There is a strong unifying factor that is present in the mentality of the people as can be found in the national motto: *Bhinneka Tunggal Ika* (Diverse, but One. Formally translated into: Unity in Diversity). Eka Darmaputera writes: "*Bhinneka Tunggal Ika*: various, yet one; diverse, but united.

This national motto does indeed represent and reflect accurately the most profound reality of the world's fifth most populous country – Indonesia. It expresses a strong desire to achieve unity despite the immense heterogeneous character of this newly built state (independent: August 17, 1945.) And the existence of this common will in its turn presupposes the existence of common cultural characteristics underlying the apparent heterogeneity" (Darmaputera 1988, 19).

He is arguing for the presence of a common cultural characteristic that has been a primary characteristic of the Indonesian people in the shape of this common will for unity and harmony amidst the diversity of its context. For Darmaputera, the characteristics of Indonesia's cultural identity can be described as follow: "... the social structure is characterized by the existence of a closely united religious agrarian community called *desa*; the religious belief is animistic; the social attitude is communalistic strongly bound by the preservation of customary law (*adat*); and the most cherished social values are mutual aid (*gotong-royong*) and *musyawarah untuk mufakat* (consultation for reaching unanimous consensus) aimed at preserving the internal harmony of the community" (Darmaputera 1988, 63).

Before the arrival of foreign colonizers, there has never been one common political administration in the region that is now Indonesia. There were certainly many kingdoms and states, but never as one unified entity. It was the occupation of the Netherlands and then the Japanese during World War II that played a major role in defining the political borders of the present Indonesia. However, in terms of identity, there is something that unites the region. SarDesai refers to it as "a massive body of indigenous civilization" (SarDesai 1997, 43). And this indigenous civilization is still working in the background of Indonesian society, shaping the ethos that allowed unity in diversity to be possible in Indonesia.

Darmaputera and SarDesai are both referring to the same abstract notion of Indonesian harmonious spirit of life, which could be found in various expressions of Indonesian communal life. Communal life in Indonesia is characterized by *gotong royong* (mutual help or the sharing of burdens) and *musyawarah untuk mufakat* (deliberation to reach consensus). The two are the most cherished social values in Indonesian society (cf. Darmaputera 1968, 63ff.). While *gotong royong* is limited more to physical activities, *musyawarah untuk mufakat* deals with all matters of decision-making and conflict resolving. They are vital in order to attain the state of *rukun,* the ideal harmonious condition for Indonesian society.

In talking about this Indonesian model of communal life, also in relation to the consensus model of decision-making, it is important to note that it requires a whole different set of skills to operate. For the Indonesian society – and also the Reformed churches in Indonesia, the 'spirit of unity' that is working in the background of the people's mindset could be summarized in the following concepts:

1. The 'Neither-Nor' paradigm
2. Gotong-royong
3. Musyawarah untuk mufakat

1. The 'Neither-Nor' Paradigm

Perhaps it is one of the most interesting characters of Indonesian society that it doesn't fit in the usual 'either-or' or 'both this-that' paradigm. For example: in describing something, we often use the paradigm of 'either-or' or 'both this and that'. In coming to a decision, whether in a synod meeting, or a civil court, the mode for decision-making usually will choose either 'yes' or 'no', 'right' or 'wrong, 'pro' or 'against'. In processes like this, we have to realize the fact that in the background there lays a process of creating an imaginary duality, or perhaps some clear polarity before then going forward and discussing what position is considered to be correct. There should be a clear distinction between 'A' and 'B', this is what is meant by the 'either-or' paradigm. Another model is the 'both this-that' paradigm. When my wife ask me to choose which dress suits her the best, my answer would usually be using this model: "both the black dress and the blue dress suit you nicely". But there is something more in the Indonesian cultural paradigm that doesn't fit within the two previous model, and this is what I refer to as the 'neither-nor' paradigm.

One example could be found in the genre of Indonesian popular folk music: the *keroncong* and the *dangdut*. The roots of *keroncong* music is brought by Portuguese sailors to Indonesia in the 16th century, and later was assimilated by upper-class citizens of the time. It is a small orchestra consist of, typically, two ukuleles, a cello, a guitar, and a bass, and accompanied by a soloist. It is basically a musical tradition of Indonesia that is being applied to an orchestra of European instruments (see Kroncong 2018). One time I stumbled upon a Portuguese musical genre, the *Fado*, and felt a strange familiarity with the music. And I was suddenly reminded by the *Keroncong*. Moved by the strange familiarity, I then did a little internet research and learned that plausibly *Fado* was the musical genre that most sailors brought to the Indonesian archipelago and was then transformed by Indonesian musicians into *Keroncong*. The present form of *Keroncong*, with its many variations, does not always sound similar to *Fado*, but when you listen and compare the two, you will find elements of *Fado* in the *Keroncong*. In other words, the *Keroncong* is not *Fado*, nor Portuguese, it is something else. It is Indonesian. The same goes with *dangdut*, which is often associated with music of the Indonesian lower-class people. It is derived from Hindustani, Malay, and Arabic music. When one listen to *dangdut*, one would feel a sense of Indian influence in the harmony, instrument, beat, and rhythm. But it is neither Indian, nor an adaptation if Indian music to Indonesia only. It is Indonesian. Both *Keroncong* and *dangdut*, they embrace their origins, but without accepting all of them. They neither reject nor accept them fully. As Darmaputera puts it: "It accepts all but does not let them stay in their original forms. It accepts all by transforming them and including them into its own system" (Darmaputera 1968, 65). Raden Mas Sutjipto Wirjosuparto gives a similar opinion regarding this Indonesian cultural identity: "Even by contact with foreign culture, the patterns of Indonesia's culture remained the same, because the foreign cultural elements were absorbed into the patterns of Indonesia's culture" (quoted in: Sumihe 2001, 86).

What we see here is a complex mindset that cannot be simply described by a general typology, or simply combining everything: it is something else. It's neither 'either-or', nor 'both this-and that'. It is something Indonesian.

2. The 'Gotong-Royong' practice

The term *gotong-royong* can be translated into 'mutual aid', 'working together', or 'cooperation'. But it isn't simply a model for getting this done; it is the appropriate method for getting everything done. In traditional Indonesian villages, weddings, *syukuran* (a thanksgiving ceremony for special occasions), funerals, etc. are done not only by the respective family but by the whole village. And that practice is still held in most Indonesian villages until today.

I remember when I had just started becoming a pastor for a congregation in a small village in Lampung, Sumatera. One of my neighbors invited me to come to their daughter's wedding celebration, which was to be held a week from then. Their house was just across the parsonage (In Indonesian: *pastori*) where I lived. But already from three to four days before the wedding day, every day – mostly in the afternoon – people would come and work on the festivities. They brought sacks of rice, sugar, palm sugar, vegetables, life chickens, coffee beans, tea, cigarettes, anything they had at hand. The men would build up open air tents, set up the stage, paint the decorations, and the women would make handicrafts from leaves and flowers, some would be in the kitchen cooking meals for everyone who was working. Some youths were sent to deliver invitations to relatives in other villages, some helped with the chores inside the house. Later in the evening, after the *maghrib* prayers, the people would usually came back and have a cozy time while trying to figure out whatever else they could contribute. Some would be talking with the family, some would just sit outside on long wooden benches sipping coffee or tea, play dominos, whatever thing they could spend their time with. In this kind of event, it wasn't so much about the number or the difficulty of the task that you are able to do; simply by being present there one is considered as taking part in *gotong-royong*. For Indonesian villages, special occasions like a wedding or a funeral can never be limited only to a family celebration: it is the celebration of the whole village. Not taking part in it, unless you have a very strong reason – or a clever excuse – would be considered as disinterest toward being part of the society. You are only a part of the society, if you are willing to participate in *gotong-royong*.

From a modern urbanized society's perspective, this method might be considered as somewhat inefficient and ineffective. But that doesn't mean that modern Indonesians reject the whole idea of *gotong-royong*. What then happens in Indonesian cities is that we find different expression of doing *gotong-royong* in the community: residential areas in cities routinely organize a *gotong-royong* in the form of cleaning the neighborhood trenches, parks, roads together. People would bring snacks, cold drinks, their cleaning equipment, etc. The head of the *rukun tangga* usually coordinates all this. Formally abbreviated as RT: *rukun* means harmonious, and *tangga* is from the term *tetangga* or neighbors. It is the smallest formal unit of community recognized by the government, even though the organization of RT is completely informal. In other words, it is the direct synonym of being a village in the urban setting.

This is *gotong-royong*, not merely how people do things together, but this sense of attachment to community life through participation in daily activity. This is another cultural aspect of being Indonesian.

3. The 'musyawarah untuk mufakat' model

The term is composed from two key concepts, *musyawarah,* an Indonesian term for deliberation or consultation, and *mufakat,* an Indonesian term for consensus or common consent. The term itself originates from the Arabic word *syawara,* but the Indonesian people practiced the concept many years before Islam arrived in the archipelago (cf. Priyotamtama 2015, 99f.). In its usage, the term is used for both a method and a principle wherein deliberation to achieve a consensus is regarded as the highest norm for coming to a decision within Indonesian society. Not every *musyawarah* process will finally come to a *mufakat,* certainly. However, the desire for consensus serves as a beacon that guides the whole process of decision-making, which transforms the process beyond winning or losing (cf. Surjanegara 2008, 9). There is no point in *musyawarah,* when there is no desire for *mufakat.* Darmaputera points out the dynamic in *musyawarah*: "The procedure of doing everything together based on and/or in order to reach the common consent of all is called musyawarah untuk mufakat. *Musyawarah* or consultation is universally practiced in the archipelago almost to every matter. Every member of the meeting is allowed to speak and has the right to be listened to. After prolonged giving and taking and weighing the pros and the cons, a decision – usually a compromise – is finally reached. Here no one will find all his/her wishes realized, nor will anyone find none of his/her wishes fulfilled. The 'neither-nor' principle prevails" (Darmaputera 1968, 37).

The central idea of doing *musyawarah* is that differences are recognized, and not resolved through a *win-lose* (*'either-or'*) paradigm. That is why voting in most Indonesian communities is regarded as a last resort, rather than the preferred option in decision-making. In *musyawarah,* it is necessary that the participants are willing to accept each other's differences by accepting a creative compromise; a communally agreed solution where no one finds neither all nor none of his/her wishes fulfilled. This does not mean that the outcome of a *musyawarah untuk mufakat* will simply be a compromise with the 'lowest common denominator'. An agreement with the 'lowest common denominator' would mean that all parties participating in the *musyawarah untuk mufakat* process stick to their prior position and simply agree to what is already shared with the rest of the group. There is no change of position needed in that process. That is not the case with *musyawarah untuk mufakat.* In *musyawarah untuk mufakat*, it is required that all those present move from their previous position, adding or negating something to it, until in the end they would reach a position that everybody would agree upon.

Musyawarah untuk mufakat is more than a method for decision-making. The fact that there is no clear formal procedure on how to conduct a *musyawarah* would seem unlikely for an ancient practice that is still accepted as a national norm for decision-making. In Indonesia, churches from different systems (presbyterial-synodical, episcopal, and congregational) also acknowledge *musyawarah untuk mufakat* as their way of coming to decisions, although they don't specifically formulate what they mean by it (cf. Darmaputera 1968, 49). This indicates, however abstract the concept is, that it still serves as a symbol expressing that desire for unity, balance, and harmony in communal life.

We can see that negotiating this delicate process of coming to a decision requires a set of skills different from that in the voting method. For a leader of the *musyawarah* to function means having the ability to recognize the core issue from each of the conflicting parties and to propose a creative compromise that enables everyone involved in the process to see it from a different and more communally consented perspective. The leader serves more as a moderator. That is why the key aspect of leading a *musyawarah* is *kebijaksanaan* (wisdom); as the fourth principle in *Pancasila,* the nation's ideology states it: *"Kerakyatan yang dipimpin oleh hikmat kebijaksanaan dalam permusyawaratan perwakilan"*, or loosely translated: Peoplehood guided by the spirit of wisdom through representation. Wisdom, however abstract, is real and recognized by a community. In a system where voting is strongly avoided, persuading into a compromise through wisdom is vital. Soemarsaid Martono explains wisdom as: "*Kebijaksanaan* (*ras*:

wisdom in employing the 'neither-nor' paradigm) refers to 'the greatest skill not only in weighing subtly the possible advantages or disadvantages of one's decision but also a keen sense of judgement in the handling of situations, primarily to preserve the cosmic order. In practice it means: a policy of checking and balancing, avoiding those disturbing open clashes that were not absolutely necessary''' (quoted in: Darmaputera 1968, 49).

All these concepts: *musyawarah untuk mufakat, gotong royong, rukun,* and *kebijaksanaan* are integral expressions of that spirit of creating and preserving unity, balance, and harmony. They are distinguishable, but not separable. And these values played a major role in keeping the present democratic republic of Indonesia united as a nation.

Sharing the Indonesian experience: Pancasila as a creative compromise

The three concepts I mentioned above: the 'neither-nor' paradigm, the '*gotong royong*' practice, and the '*musyawarah*' model, are not exclusive notions but rather expressions of a common ideal: unity. In the history of Indonesia as a nation, this ideal was later formulated and proposed in a creative compromise that became the formal principle of the Indonesian state: *Pancasila.* We can see even from the outset of its birth, the role of the cultural characteristics I mentioned earlier.

The *musyawarah untuk mufakat* ethos plays an important role in the period of Indonesia's struggle for independence, especially during the process of determining the new Indonesia's state ideology. On 28th of April 1945, a committee named *Badan Untuk Menyelidiki Usaha-usaha Persiapan Indonesia Merdeka* (The Investigating Body for the Preparation for an Independent Indonesia) was formed. The purpose of this Investigating Body was to consider the basic questions and to draft major plans for an independent state of Indonesia. During the meetings of the Investigating Body – there were two meetings, the first was from May 29 to June 1, and the second one from July 10 to July 17 – the biggest issue they had to discuss was the following question: "What is the basis or the foundation of the Indonesian state which we are about to form?" (Darmaputera 1968, 148f.; see SarDesai 1997, 172f.).

In these meetings, the struggle for what would be the base ideology of the new Indonesian state took place. Darmaputera notes: "On June 1, 1945, after three days of 'sharp conflict', Sukarno delivered his famous speech, which from then on was known as *Lahirnya Pancasila* (The Birth of *Pancasila*). In this speech he proposed a compromise: *Indonesia Merdeka* would neither be an Islamic nor a secular state, but a *Pancasila* state. According to Sukarno, *Pancasila* – literally means 'five pillars' or 'five principles' – consisted of the following principles, arranged in the following order:

1. Kebangsaan Indonesia (Indonesian Nationhood, or, Indonesia Nationalism)
2. Internasionalisme/Perikemanusiaan (Internationalism/Humanitarianism)
3. Mufakat/Demokrasi (Unanimous Consensus/Democracy)
4. Kesejahteraan Sosial (Social Welfare)
5. Ketuhanan Yang Maha Esa (The One Lordship)" (Darmaputera 1968, 150; see SarDesai 1997, 172f.).

SarDesai gives a brief explanation of *Pancasila*, or the five principles as mentioned by Sukarno: "Nationalism involved the establishment of one national state based on the entity of one Indonesian soil from the tip of Sumatra to Irian, a means of promoting unity through diversity. Internationalism would seek to establish a family of nations, with each one recognizing its respective nationalism. Though details were left to be worked out, the importance of the principles of consent, representation, and consultation to the strength of the Indonesian state was recognized. The principle of social justice underlined a political-economic democracy in which all people would prosper. And finally, Sukarno emphasized the right of every Indonesian to believe in his or her own particular God, which amounted to secularism" (Sardesai 1997,173).

This formulation of *Pancasila*, a proposal from Sukarno, emerged after a 'sharp conflict' between the two major powers at that moment, the Nationalist side and the Islamic side. The Islamic side defended the idea of Islam to be the basis of *Indonesia Merdeka* (Independent Indonesia), and the Nationalist side strongly rejected that idea in favor of a secular basis of the state (cf. Darmaputera 1968, 149). This polarization created a deadlock in the meeting. There were also some other conflicting ideas during the debates in the Investigating Body, but they were relatively minor in comparison to the polarization of those who proposed Islam and those who preferred secular principles as the foundation for *Indonesia Merdeka* (cf. Darmaputera 1968, 49). The negative consequences of both options are, as Darmaputera notes: "What was at stake here was the very identity of Indonesia: its unity and its diversity. Had the idea of a religious state prevailed, then the result would have been separation of the country into two or more states along the lines of what happened with India and Pakistan. But had the other option won, i.e., if Indonesia had become a secular state, then the diversity of Indonesia would be taken into account but without a sufficient unifying factor to make Indonesia united as a nation" (Darmaputera 1968, 149f.).

The question of what Indonesia's state ideology would be was a very crucial question that could not be resolved simply by means of voting. To determine the answer through voting would only generate a sense of *winners* and *losers*, which would further emphasize the polarization in the new state. That was the major reason why the Investigating Body accepted Sukarno's proposal of *Pancasila* immediately, since it managed to be the "middle-way in order to achieve and to preserve harmony and balance" (Darmaputera 1968, 165). It is easily accepted by both sides in conflict because, as Darmaputera puts it, "The solution offered by *Pancasila* is something that is able to avoid, or more correctly to go beyond, this 'either-or' choice" (Darmaputera 1968, 183). As a follow up to Sukarno's speech about *Pancasila*, an Ad-Hoc Committee (*Panitia Kecil*) was formed to reformulate *Pancasila* – based on the speech given by Sukarno – as the foundation of the State. This *Panitia Kecil* then formulated the text of *Piagam Jakarta* (the *Jakarta Charter*) that revised the formulation of *Pancasila* into:

1. (The principle of) One Lordship, with the obligation to carry out the Islamic syari'a for its adherents;
2. A Just and Civilized Humanity;
3. The Unity of Indonesia;
4. (The principle of) Peoplehood Guarded by the Spirit of Wisdom in Deliberation and Representation;
5. Social Justice (cf. Darmaputera 1968, 151f.).

We can see the change of order of the principles in *Pancasila*, whereas the principle of One Lordship (*Ketuhanan Yang Maha Esa*) becomes the first and guiding principle to which the other principles are subordinated (cf. Darmaputera 1968, 152). This has to be seen in the light of the efforts to neutralize the tension between the Nationalist and Islamic side, as Dharmaputera describes it: "First of all, it is very clear that *Pancasila* was proposed and accepted as a compromise between those who were in favor of a religious state and those who preferred a secular state. In this respect, the formulation of the first principle was crucial. It tried to satisfy both parties, while at the same time it could not accept any of those ideas in their entirety" (Darmaputera 1968, 153).

But this compromise was not accepted by all either, particularly concerning the emphasis on the first principle "with the obligation to carry out the Islamic *syari'a* (Islamic Law) for its adherents". Finally, during the preparation to formulate a Constitution for Indonesia, a breakthrough came that changed the *Piagam Jakarta* formulation of *Pancasila*: "... the serious objection from those whose religion was not Islam. According to them, it was inappropriate if within a principal statement which concerned the whole nation there was a regulation which was applied only to a particular part of the whole Indonesian people, even though that part was the biggest part (...) In order to guard the unity and the harmonious totality of the entire Indonesian territory, the phrase 'with the obligation to carry out the Islamic *syari'a* for its adherents' was omitted from the Preamble of the Constitution"(Darmaputera 1968, 151).

In its final form, *Pancasila* as a state ideology is formulated in the Preamble of the 1945 Constitution of Indonesia, as follows:

1. Ketuhanan Yang Maha Esa / (The Principle of) One Lordship
2. Kemanusiaan yang Adil dan beradab / (A) just and civilized humanity
3. Persatuan Indonesia / (The) Unity of Indonesia
4. Kerakyatan yang dipimpin oleh hikmat kebijaksanaan dalam permusyawaratan/perwakilan / (The Principle of) Peoplehood which is guarded by the spirit of wisdom in deliberation/representation
5. Keadilan Sosial / (Social Justice) (see Darmaputera 1968, 151).

A difficult problem usually arises in translating the first notion, that of *Ketuhanan yang Maha Esa*, in the English language. A study conducted by Sita Hidayah listed as many as eleven English translations for this notion that are used by the Indonesian government and scholars mainly from a Muslim or Christian background: 1. Belief in God; 2. The belief in one God; 3. Belief in the oneness of God; 4. Belief in the one and only God; 5. Belief in divine omnipotence; 6. God's divine omnipotence; 7. Belief in an all embracing God; 8. Belief in one divine Lordship; 9. The unity of God; 10. A supreme Godhead; 11. The absolute Lordship of God (cf. Hidayah 2010, 242f.).

To fully understand the meaning of *Pancasila* we should always keep in mind the concept of unity, balance, and harmony. The five are a harmonious whole, wherein each complements but at the same time also limits the others (cf. Darmaputera 1968, 191f.).

If we assume that the many internal and external changes that have happened in the Indonesian society have made the *Pancasila* ideology simply to a nostalgia of the past, we would be mistaken. Although during the presidency era of Suharto the concept of *Pancasila* has often been used and given a narrower meaning as a tool for disciplining the people, the society's appreciation and affirmation to its principle remains. One of the reasons is because since the first time it was accepted, it was cherished not because of its status as a formal document, but rather as an 'umbrella' that unites the Indonesian culture. Darmaputera puts it like this: "*Pancasila* has been the most viable option for Indonesia, precisely because it is rooted in this 'common culture', rather than being merely a reflection of one of the cultural layers. Not only it is acceptable to all but, more than that, all of the cultural layers see themselves represented in it" (Darmaputera 1968, 198). Douglas E. Ramage's observation about the broad Indonesian acceptance of the "formulaic expression of national unity" in *Pancasila* reads: "Indonesian political discourse suggests that while authorities use *Pancasila* to restrict the permissible boundaries of political behavior, there is also unifying value in a national ideology whose appeal cross-cuts religious, ethnic, and regional affiliations" (Ramage 1997, 202). In this short description, Ramage suggests that no matter how often at times *Pancasila* has been used and 're-interpreted' by the political powers for their own interest, it still has the appeal that it 'cross-cuts' boundaries of diversity (cf. Ramage 1997, 202).

From the story of *Pancasila* in the Indonesian context, we see how the *musyawarah* principle avoided the Indonesian nation from separation by proposing a creative compromise that goes beyond a mere 'either-or' choice. It is a testimony about a willingness to take the long and tiresome road, that could only happen because there is a strong desire to achieve and preserve unity, harmony, and balance.

Reflections

From the Indonesian experience of living out a love for unity, what can we learn in our discussion regarding church unity? These are some of my reflections:

When we are truly committed to unity, separation is never an option. This is especially true when we learn from church history. When churches came to realize that how we decide on difficult matters should not betray our unity as a church, should that not also be reflected in how we make use of the current methods that we employ? The consensus method, the *musyawarah* model, and many other similar examples could be found in the worldwide network of churches. But the main idea should not be about changing methods, rather it should be about changing the mindsets and developing a new paradigm of coming to decision as churches (see also: Surjanegara 2014, 68–69).

When I make use of the Indonesian context as an example, the intention was never about describing the details. There are many details still lacking in the Indonesian *musyawarah* model, and in many cases of church decision-making in Indonesia the term was used more as a 'lip service' rather than truly being lived out as a spirit of unity. This is the sad and fragile unity that the churches have to deal with, especially in the face of difficult contemporary issues. As we want to be decisive as churches, so often we are tempted to be divisive. Therefore, my sharing is simply a reminder that we should not give in to the easy way out: the divisive way. Rather, churches have to have the willingness and endurance in finding creative compromises to answer new challenges that threaten our unity. We don't vote out the things that we dislike, as we don't amputate the body parts that we don't like.

Because we are one body of Christ, so let the Spirit guide us to remain as one church amidst our differences and enlighten us to reflect that unity through our decision-making processes.

Abbreviations and bibliography

UCA: Uniting Church of Australia
WCC: World Council of Churches
WCC-COP: Final Report of the Special Commission on Orthodox Participation in the WCC. WCC Document no. PB-3. Accessed February 4, 2018. http://www.oikoumene.org/en/resources/documents/assembly/porto-alegre-2006/3-preparatory-and-background-documents/final-report-of-the-special-commission-on-orthodox-participation-in-the-wcc.html

Best, Thomas, and Günther Gassmann (eds.). 1994. On the way to fuller Koinonia. Official report of the fifth World Conference on Faith and Order, Santiago de Compostela 1993. Geneva: WCC Publications.
Cooley, Frank L. 1968. Indonesia: Church & Society. New York: Friendship Press.
Darmaputera, Eka. 1968. Pancasila and the search for identity and modernity in Indonesian society. Leiden: E.J. Brill.
Gassman, Günther. 1994. Montreal 1963 – Santiago de Compostela 1993: report of the director. In: Best and Gassman 1994, 12–18.
Hidayah, Sita. 2010. Translating 'Ketuhanan yang maha esa'. An amenable religious appeal. Re-legitimizing Indonesia's founding ethos. Yogyakarta: Indonesian History Studies Center – Sanata Dharma University.
Janssen, Allan J. and Leo J. Koffeman (eds). 2014. Protestant church polity in changing contexts. Ecclesiological and historical Contributions. Proceedings of the International Conference, Utrecht, The Netherlands, 7–10 November 2011. Volume I. Series: Church Polity and Ecumenism: Global Perspectives 2. Zürich: LIT-Verlag.
Koffeman, Leo J. 2001. The urge for unity. In: Koffeman and Witte 2001, 69–93.
Koffeman, Leo J. and Henk Witte (eds.). 2001. Of all times and of all places: Protestants and Catholics on the Church local and universal. Series: IIMO Research Publication 56. Zoetermeer: Meinema.
Koffeman, Leo J. and Johannes Smit (eds). 2014. Protestant church polity in changing contexts. Case studies. Proceedings of the International Conference, Utrecht, The Netherlands, 7–10 November 2011. Volume II. Series: Church Polity and Ecumenism: Global Perspectives 3. Zürich: LIT-Verlag.
Kroncong. 2018. Accessed February 4, 2018. https://en.wikipedia.org/wiki/Kroncong.
Priyotamtama SJ., Paulus Wiryono. 2015. Musyawarah and democratic lay Catholic leadership in Indonesia: the ongoing legacy of John Dijkstra, SJ, and Ikatan Petani Indonesia. In: Schuck and Crowley-Buck 2015, 99–109.
Ramage, Douglas E. 1997. Politics in Indonesia: democracy, Islam and the ideology of tolerance. London: Routledge.
SarDesai, Damodar R. 1997. South East Asia: past & present. Colorado: Westview Press.
Schuck, Michael Joseph and John Crowley-Buck (eds.). 2015. Democracy, culture, Catholicism: voices from four continents. Oxford: University Press.

Small, Joseph D. 2014. The democratic captivity of the Church. In: Janssen and Koffeman 2014, 49–63.

Sumihe, Sostenes. 2001. Injil, kebudayaan dan ideologi Pancasila: pendekatan ekumenis terhadap kebudayaan dan ideologi serta maknanya bagi gereja-gereja di Indonesia. Jakarta: Sekolah Tinggi Teologi Jakarta.

Surjanegara, Roy A. 2008. Musyawarah untuk mufakat: a contribution to the Indonesian Churches' search for unity through decision-making. Master Thesis – PThU Kampen. [Unpublished].

Surjanegara, Roy A. 2014. Being presbyterial-synodical in the changing landscape of the Reformed churches in Indonesia: responses to a problematic past and present. In: Koffeman and Smit 2014, 59–69.

Tabart, Jill. 2003. Coming to consensus: a case study for the churches. Geneva: WCC Publications.

UNITY IN MISSION:
TOWARD POST-DENOMINATIONALISM?

Leo J. Koffeman

Introduction

All churches, including those in Europe and North America, nowadays live in a missionary situation. What is the impact this has on our understanding of unity? In this contribution, I will start with a few words on the ecumenical discussion on ecclesiology, and then I will explore shortly the roman catholic approach as a background for some reflections on unity in the Reformed tradition. This will bring me to the issue of post-denominationalism and the need for a different approach of church unity.

'The Church'

It is no surprise that the important Faith and Order text *The Church: Towards a Common Vision* (2013; from here: CTCV) spends quite a few words on the issue of the unity of the church. Unity is no less than the core business of the World Council of Churches and its Commission on Faith and Order. The aim of the Commission is "to proclaim the oneness of the Church of Jesus Christ and to call the churches to visible unity in one faith and one eucharistic fellowship, expressed in worship and in common life in Christ, through witness and service to the world so that the world may believe" (By-laws of Faith and Order, reprinted in: Best 2005, 450; cf. Article 3 of the constitution of the World Council of Churches). Promoting the unity of the churches, i.e. "overcoming any remaining obstacles to their living out the Lord's gift of communion" (CTCV, Introduction) is the very goal of this ecclesiological convergence text. From the outset, unity is seen from the perspective of the mission of the Church.

CTCV opens with a chapter under the heading 'God's Mission and the Unity of the Church'; it explores how the Christian community finds its origin in the mission of God for the saving transformation of the world: "The Church is essentially missionary, and unity is essentially related to this mission" (CTCV, Introduction).

Statistically, the term 'unity' is used 91 times in the document, and in addition the number 'one' appears 118 times. Of course, CTCV refers to the last words of the Risen Lord in Matthew 28,16–20: "This command by Jesus already hints at what he wanted his Church to be in order to carry out this mission. It was to be a community of witness, proclaiming the kingdom which Jesus had first proclaimed, inviting human beings from all nations to saving faith. It was to be a community of worship, initiating new members by baptism in the name of the Holy Trinity. It was to be a community of discipleship, in which the apostles, by proclaiming the Word, baptizing and celebrating the Lord's Supper, were to guide new believers to observe all that Jesus himself had commanded" (CTCV, §2). CTCV then gives a fair account of the pros and cons of the mission history of the churches, as well as of the challenges churches face today. It includes a relevant reference to the way secularization challenges the church's self-understanding and mission: "The advance of a global secular culture challenges the Church with a situation in which many question the very possibility of faith, believing that human life is sufficient unto itself, without any reference to God. In some places, the Church faces the challenge of a radical decline in membership and is perceived by many as no longer relevant to their lives" (CTCV, §7). It is against this background that the need for church unity is stressed at the end of this chapter. It is expressed like this: "Visible unity requires that churches be able to recognize in one another the authentic presence of what the Creed of Nicea-Constantinople (381) calls the 'one, holy, catholic, apostolic church'. This recognition, in turn, may in some instances depend upon changes in doctrine, practice and ministry within any given community. This represents a significant challenge for churches in their journey toward unity" (CTCV, §9).

In the second chapter of CTCV, the ecclesiological foundation of this document is being laid. The Church is understood from a Trinitarian perspective. First, believers are united with Jesus Christ through the Holy Spirit, and thereby they share a living relationship with the Father. This is implied in the biblical notion of *koinonia*, a multilayered concept: "The noun *koinonia* (communion, participation, fellowship, sharing), which derives from a verb meaning 'to have something in common,' 'to share,' 'to participate,' 'to have part in' or 'to act together,' appears in passages recounting the sharing in the Lord's Supper (cf. 1 Cor. 10:16–17), the reconciliation of Paul with Peter, James and John (cf. Gal. 2:9), the collection for the poor (cf. Rom. 15:26; 2 Cor. 8:3–4) and the experience and witness of the Church (cf. Acts 2:42–45)" (CTCV, §13). It has become central in the ecumenical ecclesiological quest, and it forms the background of other biblical images of the Church, as the prophetic, priestly and royal people of God, the body of Christ, and the Temple of the Holy Spirit.

In the final passages on the Church as *koinonia* the Nicene attributes 'one, holy, catholic, and apostolic' are given new attention. These attributes "which are not separate from one another but which inform one another and are mutually interrelated, are God's gifts to the Church which believers, in all their human frailty, are constantly called to actualize" (CTCV, §22). It is this dialectical relationship of gift and calling that also determines the thrust of what CTCV says about the unity of the Church: "The Church is one because God is one (cf. John 17:11; 1 Tim. 2:5). In consequence, the apostolic faith is one; the new life in Christ is one; the hope of the Church is one. Jesus prayed that all his disciples be one so that the world might believe (cf. John 17:20–21) and sent the Spirit to form them into one body (cf. 1 Cor. 12:12–13). Current divisions within and between the churches stand in contrast to this oneness; 'these must be overcome through the Spirit's gifts of faith, hope, and love so that separation and exclusion do not have the last word'. Yet, in spite of all divisions, all the churches understand themselves as founded in the one gospel (cf. Gal. 1:5–9), and they are united in many features of their lives (cf. Eph. 4:4–7)" (CTCV, §22).

However, the document does not really provide more specific insights into what exactly should be the basis of visible unity in terms of the structure of the churches. It certainly contains some beautiful passages on unity and diversity (particularly in CTCV, §28–30; cf. §12), culminating in a rather dramatic and challenging conclusion: "Though all churches have their own procedures for distinguishing legitimate from illegitimate diversity, it is clear that two things are lacking: (a) common criteria, or means of discernment, and (b) such mutually recognized structures as are needed to use these effectively. All churches seek to follow the will of the Lord yet they continue to disagree on some aspects of faith and order and, moreover, on whether such disagreements are Church-divisive or, instead, part of legitimate diversity. We invite the churches to consider: what positive steps can be taken to make common discernment possible?" (CTCV, §30 comm). In other words: church unity is hampered by the absence of common criteria and the non-existence of common structures that make it possible to apply such criteria together. So, which are the criteria we can use, and which we can offer to the wider ecumenical movement in order to distinguish legitimate from illegitimate diversity, and, therefore, to help build a common basis for structural unity?

Three bonds

Roman Catholic tradition has a clear answer to this question. It speaks of a threefold bond that is decisive of full visible unity. It is the three bonds of faith, sacramental life and hierarchical ministry (reflected in the ordained ministry's threefold task of teaching, sanctifying and ruling) that together determine full membership in the visibly one church. In its Constitution on the Church, the Second Vatican Council says: "They are fully incorporated in the society of the Church who, possessing the Spirit of Christ accept her entire system and all the means of salvation given to her, and are united with her as part of her visible bodily structure and through her with Christ, who rules her through the Supreme Pontiff and the bishops. The bonds which bind men to the Church in a visible way are profession of faith, the sacraments, and ecclesiastical government and communion" (LG, §14). The issue is taken up again in the Decree on Ecumenism: Christ "perfects His people's fellowship in unity: in their confessing the one faith, celebrating divine worship in common, and keeping the fraternal harmony of the family of God" (UR, §2). It is also reflected in canon 205 of the *Codex Iuris Canonici*: "Those baptized are fully in the communion of the Catholic Church on this earth who are joined with Christ in its visible structure by the bonds of the profession of faith, the sacraments, and ecclesiastical governance". The *Directory for the Application of Principles and Norms on Ecumenism* speaks of the People of God as "united in the threefold bond of faith, sacramental life and hierarchical ministry" (DE, §20; cf. §12 and 17).

So, unity is about doctrine, Eucharistic sharing and structures. In this official Roman Catholic approach, these three bonds are intricately linked: unity in doctrine is fundamental, as it includes unity in government (because the episcopal system is a doctrinal matter itself); unity in worship, eucharistic sharing, is its final consequence, and, therefore, such sharing is not possible as a regular step towards full unity. The Orthodox tradition basically shares this view. Although Old Catholic churches, Anglican churches and some Lutheran churches have a similar doctrinal view of the episcopal form of church government, they can be less strict in the way they deal with it in an ecumenical context. Old Catholics usually welcome all believers to the table of the Lord. In the *Porvoo Agreement* Anglicans and Scandinavian and Baltic Lutherans express full communion, although the unbroken apostolic succession of some of the Nordic Lutheran bishops cannot be maintained.

Most mainline Protestant churches can agree on the importance of each of these three 'bonds' as three aspects of true visible unity. In our usual vocabulary: unity is about doctrine, about sharing, and about church structures. However, Protestant churches will maintain different views as to the way they are mutually related, if compared with the roman catholic position. For them, 'eucharistic hospitality' or a joint celebration of the Lord's Supper is possible as a step towards full unity.

Forms of Unity

How is this in the mainline churches in the Reformed tradition? How important is unity in doctrine there? Traditionally, they may have had views very similar to the roman catholic approach. In the church I grew up in half a century ago, the Reformed Churches in the Netherlands, participating in Holy Supper (at least formally) fully depended on the question if you agreed with the doctrine of the church as reflected in the *Three Forms of Unity*, i.e. the *Heidelberg Catechism*, the *Belgic Confession*, and the *Dordt Canones*. The *Belgic Confession* includes some articles on the government of the church, so the order was: doctrine – government – worship.

For most Protestant Church families, formally it is still doctrine as embodied in the confessional standards that determines their concept of church unity. Although there may be a strong tendency to open the Lord's Supper for believers from other churches and traditions, church unity still depends on agreement on key doctrinal matters. In the process of unification that resulted into the birth of the Protestant Church in the Netherlands (cf. Koffeman 2014), the contents of the first article of the church order, on the confession of the church, was among the most intensively debated issues. The fact that two Lutheran confessional standards, the *Augsburg Confession* and the*Catechism of Luther*, were included in this article, raised major objections from the more conservative wing of the Reformed community, and it was presented as the most important reason for some of them not to join the united church: about 60.000 (out of a million) members of the Netherlands Reformed Church left, and formed the Restored Reformed Church. For those leaving, their loyalty to *Three Forms of Unity* excluded any other or additional confessional standard.

In Dutch church history, this emphasis on the confessional standards has played a major role in the many divisions churches had to cope with. Particularly during the first half of the twentieth century the slightest suspicion of a deviation from its wordings could cause a conflict. For instance, a debate on the possibility of a 'sleep of the soul' between death and resurrection of the believer, could be countered with a simple reference to the wording of Heidelberg Catechism, Sunday 22: "That ... my soul after this life shall be immediately taken up to Christ its Head... " (cf. Van Langevelde 2015, 457).

It is not only doctrinal issues that has divided the Reformed family in the Netherlands so deeply over the last centuries. Personal relationships and conflicts, different appreciations of the actual social and political situation and such have certainly contributed to it, but time and again doctrinal arguments were decisive in the way conflicts were dealt with. Until today, the *Dordt Canones* prohibit a unification of the Remonstrant Brotherhood with the Protestant Church in the

Netherlands. In a similar way, the formal position of the *Belhar Confession* in South Africa seems to be the main stumbling block for a full re-unification of the Dutch Reformed family of churches.

In other words, this focus on the position of doctrine as expressed in confessional standards is the main cause of 'denominationalism'. It is not exclusively typical of roman catholic or Reformed teaching, but most mainline church families take a similar position, and this is an important factor in the ecumenical impasse churches worldwide are facing. This is true for many churches in Europa and North America, and it is also true for many of the churches that were born from the mission of such churches in other continents.

It is striking that mission does not seem to be of any significance in this approach. This is certainly not to say that mainline Reformed churches have not been very active in missionary efforts: the opposite is true! But eventually they have multiplied their own approach of the issue of church unity in their missionary activities, and they have burdened their 'daughter churches' with an ecclesial identity that did not really help them to be missionary in their own contexts. They could do so, because the church was something self-evident for them, and mission was not really a priority. Things have changed!

Mission history

Mission history nevertheless also presents inspiring examples of the opposite approach: churches have united beyond traditional doctrinal divisions, because of a shared view of the missionary challenges in a postcolonial context.

In August 1947, India attained independence from the British Empire, after a struggle characterized by largely nonviolent resistance and civil disobedience. For the churches in India this implied an enormous challenge. For decades, if not centuries, they had formally functioned as parts of the 'mother churches' in the United Kingdom, Anglican, Methodist, Presbyterian, Congregationalist, Lutheran and others. Denominationalism had been the norm. What had seemed to be self-evident for so long, proved to be a major problem under postcolonial circumstances. Of course, this was not at all a new insight: church unity negotiations had started as early as 1919. But the credibility of the churches was really at stake from the very moment of national independence. In the Southern part of the country Anglicans, Methodists, Congregational, Presbyterian, and Reformed church inaugurated the Church of South India already in September 1947. In this church, the Scriptures are the ultimate standard of faith and practice.

In 1970, a similar process resulted in the birth of the Church of North India, after forty years of negotiations between six churches: the Anglican Church of India, the Methodist Church, the Council of Baptist Churches, the Church of the

Brethren, the Disciples of Christ, and the United Church of Northern India. Nowadays, the Church of South India, the Church of North India and the Mar Thoma Syrian Church of Malabar are together in the Communion of Churches in India, which represents a further step towards unity.

An even better example might be represented by the China Christian Council (CCC), as established in 1980. As it says on the website of the World Council of Churches, "the churches in China have now entered a post-denominational period. Within the CCC, institutional protestant denominations no longer exist and believers worship together. Differences in theological or liturgical background are dealt with according to the principle of mutual respect". The CCC nowadays has over 26.000.000 members. This development should be understood against a twofold background. After mission activities in the 19th century, Protestant Christianity was generally looked down upon by Chinese people as a foreign and Western religion. It was already during the famous Edinburgh Mission Conference in 1910 (usually seen as the beginning of the modern ecumenical movement) that a Chinese representative, the Rev. Cheng Ching-Yi, delivered a speech on 'A United Christian Church without Denominational Distinctions'. In addition, the victory of communism in China (1949) resulted in decades of harsh suppression and persecution of Christians, which made it even more necessary to develop an authentic form of Chinese Christianity, based on the principles of self-governance, self-support and self-propagation. As Gu Mengfei states in his historical overview: "United worship came about as a result of believers from different denominational backgrounds enjoying service and worship together in one church; this was convenient for transportation and offered commonly supported facilities; such believers formed new congregations. Although a new congregation still kept some traditions such as the different forms of baptism, ritual, etc., it gave up denominational titles and structures, and did not emphasize denominational church order or doctrine, and it never discriminated, nor did churches attack each other. United worship was initiated from the very grassroots churches in Ningbo and Wenzhou, areas in Zhejiang province, in the spring of 1958, and soon united worship was welcomed by many other churches throughout China. Since then, institutional denominational structures and systems have waned step by step nationally, regionally, provincially and locally" (Mengfei 2008, 274). In the context of the ten-year Cultural Revolution, all churches were closed, and the persecution of Christians became very violent. After 1979, churches began to reopen nationally. Since the establishment of the CCC (1980) institutional denominations have not existed officially in China. Christians of older generations may still feel connected with the heritage of particular denominations, but in general new Christians have no idea what a denomination is. As Bishop K.H. Ting said, "we Chinese Christians have chosen the road of post-denominational unity, not because we are better than anyone else, but because we live in our particular historical situation", and all in all, "we can only say that this has been a result of the leading of the Holy Spirit, who has allowed us to bathe in the ocean of God's grace" (Ting 1983, 113, quoted in: Mengfei 2008, 283).

Post-denominationalism

However, post-denominationalism is not at all an exclusively Chinese or Southern phenomenon: "The religious landscape in the U.S. is best described these days as 'post-denominational.' Post-denominational means that it is far less important whether you are Methodist or Baptist, or even Catholic, than where you fall along the continuum of fundamentalist to evangelical to progressive (liberal) to secular or unaligned" (Thistlethwaite 2008). It is how the Rev. Dr. Susan Brooks Thistlethwaite, Professor of Theology at the Chicago Theological Seminary, characterizes American Protestantism in a presentation on the faithstreet.com website. She continues: "While some faiths or denominations generally are more evangelical or more liberal, each tradition has a wide spectrum within it. If you are a liberal Christian in a conservative Protestant denomination, you may have more in common with a Reformed Jew than with the Christians in your own denomination. The shift in religious affiliation, or away from religious affiliation, has the most correlation, in my view, with that range of religious cultural assumptions than with any specific doctrine. And when people move from one affiliation to another, they are choosing a better cultural fit". Her conclusion is based on the *Religious Landscape Survey*, a sociological report on religious affiliation in the USA as published by the Pew Forum on Religion & Public Life. It is clear from this Pew study that the old denominational affiliations no longer apply.

In my view, the same applies to Europe: it is a shared cultural context rather than a doctrinal system that undergirds the unity of churches, including the Protestant Church in the Netherlands. In 2016, the sixth report on *God in the Netherlands* was published. It is a similar survey on religion in the Netherlands, based on research done every ten years. It makes it possible to compare the present church affiliation figures with those of ten, up to fifty years ago. Data are clear, and not very positive, to say the least. Over half a century the percentage of those that say to belong to a Christian church has dropped from about 67% to about 27%. Although about 64% of the Dutch population says to be raised within a Christian tradition, 59% never attends a religious worship service, and only 12% does attend on a regular basis (cf. Bernts and Berghuijs 2016, 23, 217, 222). Unfortunately, the survey does not contain data on changes in church membership, like the American Pew Study. I assume that in quantitative terms the 'circulation of the saints' does not play the same role in Europe as it does in America, but these differences may be quite relative. And I am pretty sure that 'cultural factors' are more decisive for the way most people relate to churches than confessional standards. At the level of the congregations, such factors seem to be decisive for maintaining unity. In rural areas, tradition and strong mutual personal bonds may still play a role, although these are losing weight as well. In urban areas, people tend to stick to the congregation they are part of, but they choose another congregation if they do no longer feel at home for whatever reason. Active church members that move to another city usually first visit worship services in several local congregations before they decide which congregation they will join. Liturgical preferences, worship style, but also social class and contacts over coffee after the service, and not least the presentation of the local minister will play an important role in such decisions. At least within the Protestant Church in the Netherlands, members connect to a particular congregation for such reasons.

Diversity

In my view, it is evident that the confessional basis of the Protestant Church in the Netherlands is not meaningful at all for many of its committed members. Many church-going members would not be able to mention the names of the *Three Forms of Unity* – let alone that they would be able to list the other documents as mentioned in article I of the Constitution, like the ecumenical symbols and the Lutheran confessions. It is only the strong more orthodox wing of the church that really lives with these documents, but even there many of the younger generation in fact prefer an evangelical mood rather than a confessional doctrinal approach of church life. So, the assessment of Susan Brooks Thistlethwaite about the religious landscape in the U.S. as being 'post-denominational' would be valid for the Netherlands as well. It is mainly for reasons of church politics that the church officially bases its unity on the confessional standards.

There is a rich diversity within the church, and for most of us it is not a major problem. Diversity is also facilitated at the level of church polity. The church order of the Protestant Church in the Netherlands grants the local congregations the freedom to make choices in many respects. This is true with regard to organizational issues, like the way office-bearers will be elected or the structure and regulations for the church council itself. But it also regards other issues, like the admission of children to Holy Supper, or the possibility of giving a liturgical blessing to same-sex couples. Its worship book and its songbook include many options as well: congregations can stick to the traditional Reformed liturgy, using the 17th century Dutch Bible translation and only singing the biblical Psalms, but they can also develop an ecumenical liturgical tradition, close to roman catholic liturgy, or choose for a liturgy in the atmosphere of the worldwide evangelical movement. In practice, many congregations show some hybridity in this respect.

In fact, denominationalism is losing its relevance in the Netherlands. It is only the Roman Catholic Church that has chosen to strengthen its traditional identity, limiting its ecumenical commitment to what is deemed to be possible and necessary within the supposed boundaries as set by the Vatican. We will have to wait for the impact Pope Frances can have on the future of that church.

Unity

Our churches, at least in the Northern Atlantic area, are becoming ever more post-denominational. What does this mean in terms of church polity? As I said, unity is about doctrine, about sharing, and about church structures. In practice, the emphasis is changing now. Whereas doctrine has been the decisive factor for unity, it is now first church structures that are vital for maintaining unity in diversity. In a way, church unity has become an administrative matter. In the Protestant Church in the Netherlands, representatives of very diverse congregations meet in assemblies on different levels, i.e. in the classical assemblies (a regional meeting) and in the general synod. The church order defines as one of the main responsibilities of the classical assembly: “to manifest the mutual responsibility of the congregations, among others by way of stimulating and carrying on ecclesial conversation and promoting the mutual solidarity of the congregations” (ord. 4–15–1). The same paragraph closes with the following words: “In fulfilling its mandate, the classical assembly does justice to ecclesial diversity as manifest within its geographic area”. The church order contains a similar stipulation about the general synod.

But is this indeed only a matter of administrative unity, as some would argue? Is not it rather an expression of a different concept of unity? I would rather interpret the present situation in that way. And I think that the missionary situation of our churches in the secularized context of the Netherlands is a decisive factor here. Due to secularization, the Protestant Church in the Netherlands is developing into a post-denominational church. Its Reformed and Lutheran confessional basis is less relevant than it has been for centuries. Its presbyterial-synodical structure is under discussion, with tendencies both into a more episcopal and a more congregationalist direction. Its ethos may still be quite Reformed, in its emphasis on the local expressions of the church, on the responsibility of all believers, and on processes of common decision-making. It is not so much a confessional church as it is a confessing church, and therefore a missionary church. To facilitate fresh expressions of church life on a local level, the church order has been adapted several times over the last decade. Missionary experiments have been made possible: so-called ‘missionary congregations’ can profit from particular church order regulations about leadership, including the administration of sacraments. Migrant congregations can become part of the church without having to comply with all church order stipulations.

In one of the key sentences of article I of the Constitution this missionary basis of being a confessing church is expressed like this: “Involved in God’s turning towards the world, the church, in obedience to Holy Scripture as the one source and norm of the church’s proclamation and ministry, confesses the triune God, Father, Son, and Holy Spirit” (Art. I-3). The church confesses the triune God, and it does so because of its missionary character: it is ‘involved in God’s turning towards the world’: it is the fruit and the instrument of the *missio Dei*. Now, this clause of the Constitution seems to be far more relevant for our church order framework that the next clause, which lists all confessional standards that express our historical roots.

Abbreviations and bibliography

CTCV: The Church: Towards a Common Vision. 2013. Faith and Order Paper No. 214. Geneva: WCC.

DE: Directory for the Application of Principles and Norms on Ecumenism. Accessed September 5, 2017. http://www.vatican.va/roman_curia/pontifical_councils/chrstuni/documents/rc_pc_chrstuni_doc_25031993_principles-and-norms-on-ecumenism_en.html.

LG: Lumen Gentium. Dogmatic Constitution on the Church. Accessed September 5, 2017. http://www.vatican.va/archive/hist_councils/ii_vatican_council/documents/vat-ii_const_19641121_lumen-gentium_en.html.

UR: Unitatis Redintegratio. Decree on Ecumenism. Accessed September 5, 2017. http://www.vatican.va/archive/hist_councils/ii_vatican_council/documents/vat-ii_decree_19641121_unitatis-redintegratio_en.html.

Bernts, Anton and Joantine Berghuijs (eds). 2016. God in Nederland 1966–2015. Utrecht: Ten Have.

Best, Thomas F. (ed.). 2005. Faith and Order at the Crossroads: Kuala Lumpur 2004. Faith and Order Paper No. 196. Geneva: WCC.

China Christian Council. Accessed September 5, 2017. www.oikoumene.org/en/member-churches/china-christian-council.

Chu, Theresa and Christopher Lind (eds.). 1983. A new Beginning: An international dialogue with the Chinese church. Toronto: The Canada-China programme of the Canadian Council of Churches.

Koffeman, Leo J. 2014. How the Protestant Church in the Netherlands was born. In: Plaisier and Koffeman 2014, 11–37.

Mengfei, Gu. 2008. The post-denominational era: Chinese churches on the way towards unity. In: The Ecumenical Review, 60(2008)/3, 271–287. DOI: 10.1111/j.1758-6623.2008.tb00669.x

Plaisier, Arjan and Leo J. Koffeman (eds.). 2014. The Protestant Church in the Netherlands: Church Unity in the 21st century. Stories and Reflections. Series: Church Polity and Ecumenism: Global Perspectives 4. Zürich: LIT Verlag.

Religious Landscape Survey. 2008. Accessed September 5, 2017. Pew Forum on Religion & Public Life. Accessed September 5, 2017. http://www.pewforum.org/religious-landscape-study.

Ting, Kuang-hsun. 1983. Fourteen points from Christians in the People's Republic of China to Christians abroad. In: Chu and Lind 1983.

Thistlethwaite, Susan B. 2008. The U.S. is Post-Denominational. Accessed September 5, 2017. http://www.faithstreet.com/onfaith/2008/02/27/the-us-is-postdenominational/5056.

Van Langevelde, Ab. 2015. In het klimaat van het absolute: C. Veenhof (1902–1983) Leven en werk. Barneveld: De Vuurbaak.

EXEMPLARY CHURCH POLITY IN APPEAL PROCEEDINGS

Klaas-Willem de Jong

Introduction

Some time ago a few members of the Protestant Church in the Netherlands (PCN) asked me for advice. They belong to a congregation in a village in the eastern part of the country. The council of their congregation had decided to close and sell one of the churches. The aforementioned members brought proceedings before an ecclesiastical court of law. After a procedure of more than half a year, the regional court pronounced its judgment. In most cases these courts rule in favor of the ecclesiastical body which made the decision. In this case, however, the court partly ruled in favor of the objectors, for the church council had not exercised due care in the last phase of its procedure to close the church. Although the objectors had partly won their case, they were deeply disappointed, sad and angry. They did not recognize themselves in the way the court described the substance of their case, let alone in its verdict. One of them seriously considered leaving the church.

This case illustrates the way in which appeals against decisions of ecclesiastical bodies are dealt with in the PCN, and the estrangement it often causes. In these particular proceedings only three complainants were involved. During the six years I worked as a part-time employee for a law firm which regularly dealt with ecclesiastical proceedings, I was confronted with a few cases in which larger parties formed and the unity of the congregation was seriously threatened. However, besides the unity of the church its credibility and its mission are also at stake. Events like these may lead to severe criticism both inside and outside the church. The theme of the conference, "Mission, Church Polity, and the (Dis)Unity of the Church", therefore encouraged me to reconsider the existing procedure. In this article, I will start by providing a brief overview of this procedure and its underlying principles, and then I will evaluate it. Furthermore, I will look for theological keynotes in similar fields of the existing church order of the PCN. Finally, I will propose a few alternative procedures, which in my opinion are preferable in the light of both the evaluation and the presented theological keynotes. In my line of thought I will confine myself to the ground level of the church, the local congregation.

1. The existing procedure and its underlying principles – description and evaluation

The basic rule in the church order of the PCN (PCO) regarding the procedure to file an appeal reads as follows: if someone who is entered in one of the registers of a PCN congregation objects to a decision of an ecclesiastical body, and if this decision directly affects him (or her), he (or she) is entitled to file an appeal with the appropriate ecclesiastical court (see ORD. 12–3-1). Apart from individuals, ecclesiastical bodies are also entitled to this two-stage procedure.

According to the PCN's church order, the aim of the existing procedure is to maintain justice with due observance of righteousness and love in the community of the church (see ORD. 12–1-1). In a concept of the ordinances it reads: to protect justice, righteousness and love in the community of the church (see ONTWERP, 131, at ORD. 12–1-1). In this wording justice, righteousness and love are of the same level. Unfortunately, we do not know why the wording changed (cf. Van den Heuvel 1991, 329). Strikingly, the underlying constitutional articles of the church order only mention the existence of the appeal proceedings, and no goal is given.

An ecclesiastical court may rule the appeal well-founded if it meets at least one of the following criteria (see GRKR, art. 23–1): (a) the decision has been made contrary to the church order or to legal stipulations; (b) the decision-making ecclesiastical body has not observed due care; (c) the decision-making ecclesiastical body has misused its discretionary power for a purpose other than for which it was granted; (d) the decision-making ecclesiastical body could reasonably not have made the contested decision.

These criteria are derived from the main principles of administrative law as laid down in the General Administrative Law Act. The first criterion expresses the principle of legality. The second is rooted in one of the basic provisions: "When preparing an order an administrative authority shall gather the necessary information concerning the relevant facts and the interests to be weighed" (art. 3:2 AWB). The third criterion, also known as 'détournement de pouvoir', can be found in the next provision of the same act: "An administrative authority shall not use the power to make an order for a purpose other than that for which it was conferred" (art. 3:3 AWB). Finally, the fourth criterion is linked to two related obligations: "1. When making an order the administrative authority shall weigh the interests directly involved in so far as no limitation on this duty derives from a statutory regulation or the nature of the power being exercised. 2. The adverse consequences of an order for one or more interested parties may not be disproportionate to the purposes to be served by the order" (art. 3:4 AWB). It can be noted that the order of the criteria in ecclesiastical law is the same as in secular, administrative law.

There are many compelling arguments for this approach of ecclesiastical proceedings. As a matter of principle, in a church with a presbyterial-synodical system, the assemblies of the church make the decisions. For example, in the above-described case, it is the church council which makes the decision, not the members of the congregation. Subsequently, the ecclesiastical courts restrain from any interference in the substantive considerations of an assembly. There is a practical reason for doing so. The PCN is a plural church. Although there is a common ground, the religious convictions and views of its members and congregations differ substantially. Finally, the procedure (and thus the underlying legislation) has proven itself to be legally sound; the civil courts in the Netherlands acknowledge the verdicts of the ecclesiastical courts to a very high extent (cf. Santing-Wubs 2014, Van der Ploeg 2014). In this way, the PCN can settle its own disputes, bearing in mind Paul's advice in 1 Cor. 6: 1 and 6.

Another argument for this approach can be found in the Reformed tradition. One of the founding Reformed church orders, the church order of Dordrecht (1618–19), states in article 31: "If anyone complains that he has been wronged by a decision of a minor assembly, he may appeal to a major ecclesiastical assembly" (DeRidder 1987, 550). However, there are three huge, partly related differences between the procedure described in this article and the appeal proceedings in the current church order of the PCN. According to article 31, (a) an appeal has to be submitted to a major assembly (b) which is authorized to deal with the full substance of a case, especially when points of belief and confession are at stake. Like the minor assembly, the major assembly exclusively consists of office bearers. By contrast, in the PCN (a) an appeal has to be brought before an ecclesiastical court, (b) which assesses the case minimally. An assembly appoints the members of the court, some of whom must be office bearers (see ORD. 12–2), out of the confessing members of the PCN. The third difference concerns the body that makes a decision: according to article 31, only the decision of an assembly can be subject to an appeal, whereas in the PCN the proceedings involve decisions of all ecclesial bodies of the PCN.

The creation of the independent ecclesiastical courts dates back to 1951. One of the predecessors of the PCN, the Netherlands Reformed Church, introduced a completely renewed church order in that year (see Oostenbrink-Evers 2000). The introduction of an independent juridical system was motivated by the separation of powers (cf. the *trias politica*). It was made clear in the synod that the courts should restrain from policy decisions, let alone belief statements. In practice they did restrain most of the time. Although no criteria were given in the church order of 1951, a vast majority of the cases was assessed for legitimacy, not for efficiency (see Van den Heuvel 1991, 329; Van den Heuvel 2001a, 424f; cf. also Van den Heuvel 2001, 258ff.). It seems to me that since the introduction of the church order of the PCN, probably as a result of the criteria set out in it, a minimal assessment has become common practice.

The above-mentioned differences lead me to the objections to the procedure in the PCN. I must admit that the existing procedure is a legally sound settlement of a dispute. However, in my opinion it lacks a solid theological basis. The main aim of the procedure is to maintain justice. Indubitably, justice is a biblical notion, but even as such it is a very broad concept (cf. Patte 2010, 668–675 (s.v. justice), 1078 (s.v. righteousness)). It needs focus. I presume Karl Barth can help us out here. In his *Church Dogmatics*, he speaks about church polity in the context of the doctrine of reconciliation, more specifically of the upbuilding of the Christian community. For him, church polity is principally a 'law of service'; it serves the Lord and the community (see Barth 1959, 690; cf. 695). Therefore, in my opinion, the maintenance of justice cannot be an aim in itself. In this respect, one could point at church polity as a whole, for it serves, or at least should serve, the Lord and the community. The appeal proceedings of the PCN are meant to ensure its church polity functions from a legal point of view. However, in this way justice becomes easily separated from the Lord and the community it should serve. The current church order of the PCN and the way it is interpreted and applied underline my fear of this separation. The maintenance of justice is applied narrowly. As I showed above the criteria are directly derived from secular administrative law. Hence, it is no coincidence that these criteria are laid down in the more practical general regulations of the church order instead of in the more principal-phrased ordinances of the church order. In this respect the church polity of the PCN has become far removed from the challenge Barth faced when he quoted Erik Wolf: "What might it not mean for the world if Church order and law were not merely spiritual adaptations of worldly constitutions and codes, but genuine and original witnesses to the brotherly fellowship of Jesus Christ!" (Barth 1959, 719). Barth argued for a living church law, "willing and ready for new answers (...) which have legal form and precision, although without unnecessary refinement" (Barth 1959, 711).

Subsequently, this very restricted approach probably contributes to a feeling of alienation from church and faith: a feeling of powerlessness, meaninglessness, normlessness and value isolation (see Seeman 1959). Especially the objectors can easily get the impression that they are not being taken seriously and may probably leave the community. When the media publish about the case, the public opinion will usually tend to agree with them.

Another concern is of a different nature. Most if not all disputes in appeal proceedings can be classified as conflicts between individuals and/or groups. Managing church conflict is a subject in itself. In this paper, I just refer to Hugh F. Halverstadt. In his book *Managing Church Conflict* he offers an approach to settle disputes based on the biblical term of 'shalom', peace (see Halverstadt 1991; cf. Brubaker 2009). It may be viewed as an elaboration of the aim to build up the Christian community. Halverstadt states that win/win solutions should be pursued and win/lose outcomes have to be avoided, for in the latter differences are not resolved properly. In my opinion, most rulings of ecclesiastical courts can only be described as win/lose outcomes. The underlying conflicts are only superficially dealt with. Further, any development is likely to become problematic. However, I cannot deny that in some cases a ruling puts an end to a lengthy discussion where the stakeholders themselves would never have reached a clear outcome.

2. Alternatives within the current church order

The current church order of the PCN provides suitable alternatives at different levels. The first level I want to elaborate on briefly is the aim of the proceedings before ecclesiastical courts. Next, I present the alternatives the current church order offers to the procedure itself.

2.1. The aim

The church order contains separate proceedings to manage a special category of conflicts: a set of rules for supervision and discipline. According to the ordinances in the church order, supervision and discipline have a fourfold aim, partly derived from the Reformed tradition: to build up a congregation spiritually, to preserve those going astray, to reconcile them with the congregation and their neighbors, and to maintain order in the life of congregation and church (see ORD. 10–6-1). In the underlying constitutional articles of the church order, we find the Reformed-Calvinistic threefold purpose: supervision and discipline serve the glory of God, the preservation of the congregation and the salvation of those who go astray (see PCO, art. XII-1, cf. Bouwman 1912, 172–177). The concrete criteria, however, are rather vague: an unchristian confession or way of life or another kind of disturbance of the order in life and work of the church (see ORD. 10–9-6, cf. Koffeman 2014, 76f). It will not be possible to directly apply the fourfold aim of the supervision and discipline proceedings to the appeal proceedings. Still, following the principles of Karl Barth, I am convinced that aims such as 'building up the congregation' and 'reconciliation' should be at the heart of every ecclesiastical procedure.

2.2. The procedure

At the moment, the church order offers four alternatives to the procedure. Strictly speaking, they are extra options. The first alternative is a request to the ecclesiastical body that made the decision to reconsider it (cf. PCO, art. XIV-2; ORD. 12–12; AWB, art. 7:1; Nauta 1971, 144–146). It is in churches of the Reformed tradition, especially in those which follow the Dortian church order in any form, common practice. Sometimes it is even mandatory before one is allowed to file an appeal. The ecclesiastical body is not obliged to take the request into consideration, unless an element is brought into question which was not or not sufficiently considered yet. This revision has several advantages. Filing an appeal almost always causes further estrangement. Revision can prevent the conflict from moving to the next stage where a win/lose solution becomes almost inevitable. In principle, the full substance of the case can be dealt with. It is an *ex nunc* assessment; new facts and developments can thus be taken into account too. On the other hand, one of the main disadvantages is the fact that in many cases the two parties have already ended up in a stalemate, especially when a long procedure preceded. If this is the case, both parties may lack the courage and the energy to begin a real dialogue again. In the case I presented in the introduction, the objectors had asked for such a revision. Unfortunately for them, the church council rejected the request without even considering it seriously. Perhaps a solution for this problem can be found in the introduction of a compulsory external supervisor. In that case, the procedure starts to resemble mediation. However, in the revision procedure it is the ecclesiastical body which makes the final decision.

The other alternatives can be found in one of the General Regulations of the church order, the one for appeal proceedings. In the preliminary chapter with general provisions, the regulation emphasizes that the parties involved may agree to settle their dispute through arbitration, binding advice or mediation. If they agree to do so, a court may suspend proceedings until the outcome of the alternative litigation has become clear (see GRKR, art. 1a; cf. HANDELINGEN 2012, 81–84, 88f, 91f, 125ff, 131f, 134f, 341–346). Those who introduced mediation as a suitable alternative for appeal proceedings in the PCN had an idealistic motive: they observed it as a biblical way of dealing with conflicts (see HANDELINGEN 2012, 83).

Binding advice means that a third party or one of the parties involved settles the dispute. There are a limited number of statutory provisions in Dutch law (see art. 7:900–910 BW). Therefore, it may take different forms. From the point of view of Dutch civil law, the present procedure in the PCN to deal with appeals against decisions can be considered as a form of binding advice (see Santing-Wubs 2002, 121, 176–182; cf. Santing-Wubs 2014, 178). The legal provisions for settling a dispute, though, do not affect churches. They are allowed to choose their own procedures, whether they match legal provisions or not.

Arbitration is set by Dutch civil law too (see art. 1020–1077 RV; cf. Santing-Wubs 2002, 116–121 and 126–128). Mediation is not (yet) (cf. Santing-Wubs 2002, 128–131). In all three approaches, in principle, all aspects of the disagreement can be incorporated into the handling of the case. To make use of mediation, the parties involved have to approve both the exercise of the remedy and the choice of the mediator. With respect to arbitration and binding advice, as alternatives to settle a dispute in the PCN the situation will usually be similar. Subject to certain conditions, in arbitration as a fixed procedure a church may also force an objector to challenge a decision before a council of arbitrators (as is in principle the case in the Organization of Jewish Communities in the Netherlands; cf. Santing-Wubs 2014, 172f). The church can appoint arbitrators itself, but it also can give parties the right to nominate one or more arbitrators, for example people who share their views and convictions.

3. Conclusions and suggestions

After I wrote the initial version of this paper a new development occurred. In 2016, the PCN started a thorough reorganization, called ‘Church 2025’ (see KERK2025A). The most recent proposals suggest combining the varying procedures of appeal and discipline, at least to some degree (cf. KERK2025B, esp. 38–43). One court should be established with two chambers, one for appeal proceedings and one for disciplinary cases. The foundation for this change is practical. Increasingly, discipline proceedings have the characteristics of a lawsuit. Parties often call in professional lawyers. Especially in cases of sexual abuse, the church is under serious scrutiny. Moreover, the current structure of varying procedures is complex. Because the supply of informed volunteers is expected to decrease, it is important that the presented alternative be more efficient. Strikingly, the underlying aim of the appeal proceedings is not in dispute. In my opinion, the PCN should now take the opportunity to repair the flaw in its church order. All proceedings should serve the upbuilding of the Christian community. The maintenance of law should be transformed into the maintenance of the ‘law of service’ and as such be subordinated to this main purpose.

Then, in procedures such as appeal proceedings, it makes sense to compel an objector to request a revision of the decision he opposes before he starts proceedings. In such a case, it is advisable to seek the help of a supervisor. Invoking professional help should perhaps be made compulsory.

Alternatives to ecclesiastical litigation should be promoted more widely, especially arbitration, since a compulsory request for revision makes mediation almost superfluous. It is unlikely an ecclesiastical body is willing to agree to mediation then. In mediation both parties are equal; therefore, its starting position becomes worse than in the revision procedure in which it is up to the ecclesiastical body to make the final decision.

Furthermore, I suggest two changes in the procedure as it is now. The first change relates to the application of the assessment criteria; they should be modified. According to the church order of the PCN, when certain subjects are at stake a church council has to inform and hear the congregation's opinion about its intended decision. At the moment, it is sufficient that the council has informed the congregation and offered it the opportunity to give its opinion as such (cf. ORD. 4–8-7). Piet van den Heuvel, a Dutch expert in church polity, stresses that the opinions of the members of the congregation should be given their proper weight in the decision of the church council (see Van den Heuvel 2013, 181). I would even go a little step further. Observing due care means, in my view, that the church council has to take the views and remarks of the congregation verifiably to heart (cf. De Jong 2016, 116–118). Therefore, the courts should be able to use their discretion to assess a case more substantively than they do now. This leads me to the second suggestion, which is derived from arbitration arrangements. I propose giving the parties involved a say in the composition of a part of the court; they may select one or more members of the court from a list of qualified candidates. For a sound judgment, it is necessary that at least one member of the court is able to sense the atmosphere and spirituality in which a decision has been made and has had its effect.

I am convinced these adaptations will not only strengthen the theological base of the rulings of ecclesiastical courts, but also have other advantages. They strengthen the credibility of the church, because they enable her to put her own principles of justice, righteousness and peace into effect. Subsequently, the adaptions provide the church with the opportunity to show in her own practice of appeal proceedings what her mission is about. Her church polity may become exemplary, as Karl Barth once envisioned (cf. Barth 1959, 719–726). Finally, the changes I would propose increase unity within the PCN. I am aware of the fact that these changes would subtly shift the focus of the organization from the church council to the meeting of the members of the congregation, as well as from the church council to the ecclesiastical court. For the well-being of a congregation, that does not seem to me too high a cost.

Abbreviations and bibliography

AWB: Algemene Wet Bestuursrecht (General Administrative Law Act). Texts from the AWB are cited from a translation, which can be found on an official site of the Dutch government. Accessed February, 18, 2017. https://www.rijksoverheid.nl/documenten/

besluiten/2006/06/21/engelse-tekst-awb. It seems, however, that the document from which the quotes are taken itself is not an official one.

BW: Burgerlijk wetboek (Dutch Civil Code).

GRKR: Generale Regeling Kerkelijke Rechtspraak (Provisions for Ecclesiastical Proceedings). In: PCO, 401–421.

HANDELINGEN: Handelingen [Generale Synode] Protestantse Kerk 2012. Utrecht: Protestantse Kerk in Nederland.

KERK2025A: Kerk 2025: Waar een Woord is, is een weg. January 2016. Utrecht: Protestantse Kerk in Nederland. Accessed February 18, 2017. https://www.protestantsekerk.nl.

KERK2025B: Kerk 2025: Een stap verder. April 2016. Utrecht: Protestantse Kerk in Nederland. Accessed February 18, 2017. https://www.protestantsekerk.nl.

ONTWERP: Ontwerp-ordinanties behorende bij de ontwerp-kerkorde van de Verenigde Protestantse Kerk in Nederland. 1997. Zoetermeer: Boekencentrum.

ORD: Ordinantie (ordinance). Explanatary note. The church order of the PCN, PCO, dates back to 2004 and consists of four parts. The first section ("Kerkorde", 9–24), numbered with Roman numbers, forms the foundation. It can be considered as the Constitution of the church. The second part ("Ordinanties", 27–200) contains the ordinances. The ordinances form an elaboration of the founding articles. They in particular play a major role in everyday church life. The third section ("Overgangsbepalingen", 203–267) contains a set of transitional provisions. In the fourth and most extensive part ("Generale regelingen", 203–471) a large number of practical regulations can be found, such as the GRKR.

PCN: Protestantse Kerk in Nederland (Protestant Church in the Netherlands).

PCO: Kerkorde van de Protestantse Kerk in Nederland inclusief de ordinanties, overgangsbepalingen en generale regelingen. 2013. Zoetermeer: Boekencentrum. The most recent version of the church order can be found online at www.protestantsekerk.nl.

RV: Wetboek van Burgerlijke Rechtsvordering (Code of Civil Procedure).

Balke, Willem et al. 2001. De kerk op orde? Vijftig jaar hervormd leven met de kerkorde van 1951. Zoetermeer: Boekencentrum.

Barth, Karl. 1959. Church Dogmatics. Volume IV. The Doctrine of Reconciliation. Part 2. Translated by G.W. Bromiley and T.F. Torrance. Edinburgh: T & T Clark.

Bouwman, Harm. 1912. De kerkelijke tucht naar het gereformeerde kerkrecht. Kampen: Kok.

Brubaker, David R. 2009. Promise and Peril: Understanding and Managing Change and Conflict in Congregations. Herndon (Virginia): The Alban.

De Jong, Klaas W. 2016. Zo mogelijk met eenparige stemmen. In: NTKR, Tijdschrift voor Recht en Religie 2016/2, 107–119.

DeRidder, Richard R. (ed.). 1987. The Church Orders of the Sixteenth Century Reformed Churches of the Netherlands Together with Their Social, Political, and Ecclesiastical Context. Grand Rapids: Calvin.

Halverstadt, Hugh F. 1991. Managing Church Conflict. Louisville (Kentucky): Westminster.

Koffeman, Leo J. 2014. In Order to Serve: An Ecumenical Introduction to Church Polity. Series: Church Polity and Ecumenism: Global Perspectives 1. Zürich-Berlin: LIT Verlag.

Nauta, Doede. 1971. Verklaring van de kerkorde van de Gereformeerde Kerken in Nederland. Kampen: Kok.

Oostenbrink-Evers, Hélène. 2000. Beginselen en achtergronden van de kerkorde van 1951 van de Nederlandse Hervormde Kerk. Een kerkrechtelijk onderzoek naar de structuur van de Nederlandse Hervormde Kerk, zoals die werd ontworpen door de Commissie voor beginselen van Kerkorde (1942–1944) en de Commissie voor de Kerkorde (1945–1947). Zoetermeer: Boekencentrum.

Patte, Daniel (ed.). 2010. The Cambridge Dictionary of Christianity. New York: Cambridge University Press.

Santing-Wubs, Albertha H. 2002. Kerken in geding. De burgerlijke rechter en kerkelijke geschillen. Den Haag: Boom.

Santing-Wubs, Albertha H. 2014. Geschilbeslechting binnen kerkgenootschappen. In: Van Drimmelen and Van der Ploeg 2014, 167–193.

Seeman, Melvin. 1959. On the Meaning of Alienation. In: American Sociological Review 24 (1959)/6, 783–791.

Van den Heuvel, Piet. 1991. De hervormde kerkorde: Een praktische toelichting. Zoetermeer: Boekencentrum 1991.

Van den Heuvel, Piet. 2001. De kerkelijke rechtspraak. In: Balke et al. 2001, 241–264.

Van den Heuvel, Piet. 2001a. De hervormde kerkorde. Een praktische toelichting. Second edition. Zoetermeer: Boekencentrum.

Van den Heuvel, Piet (ed.). 2013. Toelichting op de kerkorde van de Protestantse Kerk in Nederland. Zoetermeer: Boekencentrum.

Van der Ploeg, Tymen J. 2014. De verhouding tussen het interne recht van geloofsgemeenschappen en het burgerlijk recht. In: Van Drimmelen and Van der Ploeg 2014, 335–347.

Van Drimmelen, Leen C., and Tymen J. van der Ploeg (eds.). 2014. Geloofsgemeenschappen en recht. Den Haag: Boom.

THE MISSIONAL BISHOP: CLASSIS ASSEMBLY, CHURCH PLANTING AND CHURCH RENEWAL

Leon van den Broeke

Missio Dei

At the international conference on Church Polity, Utrecht in the Netherlands 2011, the South African missiologist Nelus Niemandt raised the question: "How can the missional character of the church be expressed in its polity?" (Niemandt 2014, 65). He stated: "There seems to be ecumenical consensus on the missional nature of the church – a shift from a church-centered mission to a mission-centered church" (Niemandt 2014, 67). *Missio Dei* leads to the *missiones ecclesiae*. The church is understood as missional by its very nature. Again Niemandt: "One of the most basic assertions of missional ecclesiology is that the church participates in the reality of God's presence and activity in the world" (Niemandt 2014, 69). His approach connects ecclesiology and missiology. I would like to connect them with church polity and to elaborate on this approach. This article is concerned with the interplay of missional ecclesiology and missional Reformed church polity. The last part is quite unusual. Church polity is usually regarded as focused more on the church-centered church, the inner ecclesiastical organization and its inner regulations, and less on the missional vocation of the church. This has often been the case with the central feature of Reformed church polity, the classis assembly – the board which is in charge of the regional church and its congregations, both from a supervisory (*episkopè*) and a communal (*koinonia*) point of view.

If the church is to be a missional-centered church what does that mean for what I will call missional (Reformed) church polity? Dutch missiologist Stefan Paas states that: "Mission is about the capability of the Christian faith to enter new contexts, connect different groups, inspire new generations, and impact societies. Here, a well-known paradox can be seen: innovation (renewal) cannot be planned or programmed. If you can predict what a future innovation will look like, it is no real innovation. Innovation is behind the horizon. We are looking for new answers, rather than answers we can see from where we stand" (Paas 2012, 469). If this is true, then this challenges the flexibility of Reformed church polity and its system of governance. In exploring this challenge, I will focus on the classis assembly, which consists of delegates of the consistories of local congregations in a certain region. My question is: why is it necessary that also the classis assembly should be missional in its nature? My exploration will draw on several documents and initiatives: the nature of the classis assembly; Reformed geography with a view to the regional and local levels; the relationship between classis and mission; 'Kerk 2025 (Church 2025)' – the report of the Protestant Church in the Netherlands that has consequences for the classis structure and government; a best practice: the Classis Renewal Ministry Team in the Christian Reformed Church in North America; again about the connection between classis and mission, and finally concluding remarks.

Classis assembly

Usually the classis assembly is not regarded as being involved in mission. It is associated with rules, authority, structures, ecclesial bureaucracy, and supervision. In short, something remote from the essence of the church. Both my research and experience have confirmed that the topic of the classis assembly is not popular (cf. Van den Broeke 2005; Van den Broeke 2010). On 1 April 2008, I organized, together with Allan J. Janssen (an expert in the church polity of the Reformed Church in America), an international conference on the classis and the presbytery (see Janssen and Van den Broeke 2010). There seemed to be much resemblance in the bad practices of these assemblies and judicatories. Bad practices in the classis assemblies are not limited to the Netherlands, but are also found in the North American and South African contexts. Many stories can be told about bad practice in the classis assembly or presbytery. I would like to step back from specific instances of good or bad practice and reflect on the nature of the classis assembly with a view to its mission, and look at its challenges and possibilities.

The classis assembly is the Reformed bishop, and the classis as a geographic entity of several congregations in a certain area can be considered as the Reformed bishopric. The Synod of Emden of 1571 considered the classis to be the communion of neighboring congregations (cf. Rutgers 1899, 58). The main duty of the classis assembly is the approbation of the call of a pastor (*approbatio*), visitation (*visitatio*), admonition (*admonitio*), discipline (*admonitio/ excommunicatio*), and the examination of ministers and candidates for the ministry (*examinatio*). These tasks seem to fulfill the episcopal duties. The classis assembly was formally established for the benefit of the local congregations/consistories and is to provide the consistories of the local congregations with advice. During the centuries various tasks of the classis assembly have been accented. Today in the various Reformed denominations in the Netherlands the aspect of *koinonia* – fellowship – is overemphasized. However, this could emphasize the old and still vivid ecclesiological vision of the Synod of Emden of 1571 that the classis is a community of neighboring congregations.

In 2015, the General Synod of the Protestant Church in the Netherlands (PCN) adopted by vote a synodical report called *Kerk 2025*. It was the beginning of a process in which the general synod step by step made further decisions. In this article I will include some aspects that were not yet clear at the time of the Princeton conference. *Kerk 2025* It deals with the nature and future of the church. *Kerk 2025* states that transparency, space, and simplicity are the keywords for the reorganization of the PCN. This process has two sides. On the one hand, the local church gets more space and will carry a reduced load of regulations that are not directly serving the proclamation of the gospel, community, deaconry, and mission in the world. On the other hand, we are together church, we have to take care of each other, and we have to acknowledge the fact that we testify to the gospel together in our society.

One of the implications of Kerk 2025 is an overemphasis on koinonia. At the same time the number of classis assemblies has been reduced from 76 to 11 making them significantly larger geographically. Within these larger classis assemblies there will be space for smaller entities – gatherings of congregations in a particular area. It is not quite clear what the status of these smaller entities will be. It is clear that they will not be a mandatory gathering of delegated ministers, elders, and deacons. The 'classis pastor' (see below), cooperating closely with the board of the larger classis assembly, will have a limited amount of episcopal authority. He or she will be a kind of a bishop-in-presbytery (cf. Van den Broeke 2011). However, the classis assemblies will still be involved with matters such as approval of the call or dismissal of a minister, and admonition and discipline.

'In order not to forget'

It seems that there is friction between two main aspects of the classis: *episkopè* (supervision) and *koinonia* (fellowship). Since the Synod of Emden in 1571 the classis assembly has been designed for collegial leadership. This Synod drafted an organizational plan for the Reformed church in the Netherlands. Looking backwards it seems a bit odd. It is like the plan was drawn up in the abstract, apart from grappling with details of implementation. The Synod made this draft with the sense of 'ne quid negligantur' – in order not to forget. In 1992 the Dutch pastor Bernard Luttikhuis stated in his PhD-thesis *Een grensgeval* that this draft was a pastoral plan made by the synod (cf. Luttikhuis 1992, 61f.). Despite the war with Spain and the difficult political and military situation in the Netherlands, the

Synod of Emden wanted to cover the whole territory and to make a division into classis assemblies – war or not.

Something similar happened in 1892 when two secession movements of the Netherlands Reformed Church joined forces and merged into the Reformed Churches in the Netherlands. The Acts of the new 'church' show that a division into classis assemblies was already made in advance. The list (see ACTA 1985) included the local congregations on the one hand and the provincial or particular synods on the other hand. It highlights the importance of making a pastoral-geographical division, in order to be sure that there were no 'blank spots', places in the Netherlands with no Reformed congregation. Further, the Acts state that in the sixteenth-century the Reformed church made a geographical division according to four principles: 1. to adhere to the civil geographical division; 2. to adhere to the Roman-Catholic division as in bishoprics; 3. convenience and the regional customs of the internal fellowship; 4. not too big or too small classis assemblies (see ACTA 1985).

Back to the Synod of Emden. It made a draft, a framework, for the agenda of the classis. This framework is an expression of its tasks:

- one of the pastors held a sermon. Afterwards it was discussed;
- the pastors unanimously elected a president;
- the president said a prayer;
- the president asked the delegates of the consistories of congregations whether:
    - the consistories convened;
    - admonition and discipline was maintained/executed;
    - there were problems in the congregations with heretics;
    - there were doubts about the Reformed doctrine;
    - the poor were take care of;
    - education was taken care of; and
    - consistories needed the advice of other pastors;
- the president started the discussion on one or more issues concerning the difference with Roman-Catholic doctrine, in order to edify the members of the classis;
- delegates to the provincial or particular synod were appointed: two pastors and two elders or deacons, or: one pastor and one deacon or elder;
- the acts of the previous meeting were read and discussed in order to prepare the upcoming provincial or particular synod;
- the date, time, and venue of the upcoming meeting of the classis assembly was set; and
- the president said grace.

Classis and mission

This overview shows that for the Synod of Emden and subsequently, mission was not an explicit task of the classis assembly. However, ecclesiastical practice shows that the early classis assembly was indeed involved in mission. Of course, not in this sense that former Roman-Catholic parishes became Reformed. Six classis assemblies in the Dutch Republic were involved in mission due to the work of the West Indies Company (WIC) and the United East Indies Company (VOC), in cooperation with the Admiralities: Amsterdam, Schieland or 'Maze' (Rotterdam), Walcheren, Hoorn, Enkhuizen ('Noorderkwartier'), and Groningen ('Stad en Lande'). These classis assemblies were the center of a global Reformed and maritime network: in the East, the West, and the 'Rest'. To the East belonged: The East Indies, China, Japan, India, Thailand, Ceylon. To the West belonged: North and South America, West and South Africa. To the 'Rest' belonged Germany, Poland, Russia, and the navy. The six classis assemblies appointed the so-called 'deputies for maritime affairs' to carry out the work connected with overseas congregations. They formally established overseas congregations, maintained contact by correspondence, examined comforters of the sick. The classis assembly examined ministers, and if it was a candidate for the ministry the classis assembly ordained him after his examination. For the benefit of the overseas congregations the deputies maintained contact with the directors of the VOC and the WIC. Many of these congregations still exist.

Not only abroad, but also within the Netherlands the church was involved in mission. The Reformed Churches in the Netherlands, a merger (1892) of two groups of Seceders who had left the Netherlands Reformed Church in 1834 and 1886 respectively became quite active in inner mission. For example, the first congregation I served as a minister, Bakkeveen in the province of Friesland (North-Eastern part of the Netherlands), was formally established in 1959 by the Classis Assembly of Drachten. Although it was not an official task of the classis assembly to play a role in mission work, it *was* an official task to formally establish local congregations. The formal establishment of the *Gereformeerde Kerk van Bakkeveen* (Reformed Church of Bakkeveen), and of many others, was a result of the youth ministry and evangelization work that the Classis Assembly of Drachten had engaged in beginning in the 1920s and 1930s. Responding to the context of high unemployment, alcoholism, and poverty, the classis assembly considered it as its duty to take care of the regional society and to spread the Reformed doctrine and way of life. Moreover, as soon as there were enough candidates for eldership and the diaconate, and there was support from neighboring churches, the classis assembly instituted a new congregation. That was the goal, however small the new congregation might be. Sometimes it required only one elder and one deacon to establish a new congregation. Some of these congregations survived, others remained or became too vulnerable and were disestablished, or merged with neighboring congregation(s).

Between 1892 and 1992, 417 congregations were formally established in the Reformed Churches in the Netherlands (see: GP 1992). Of course, in many cases this was the result of the expansion of a village or city, a merger or division of already existing congregations and therefore not a result of missionary work. Nonetheless, in some cases the formal establishment of such a congregation was the result of evangelization and/or youth ministry. Apart from the abovementioned seventeenth- and twentieth-century examples of missionary work, the classis assemblies were also involved in sending out ministers for the mission work – either home or foreign mission. This established a bond between both parties during the years of the assignment. The missionary sent letters and reports about the work to the classis assembly. The latter organized meetings when the missionary was back for a holiday. Also the local congregations in the classis organized meetings, because of this connection. They raised money, hosted the missionary when he or she was home, prayed for him or her, and sent letters.

Kerk 2025

Though a neglected aspect of the classis assembly, home and foreign mission sheds light on the nature of the classis assembly. Its nature is not only *episcope* and *koinonia*, but also *missio Dei*. Recovery of this aspect of the classis assembly would be useful for the church of today and of the future. In a secularized context, denominations are more aware of the fact that the nature of the church is *missio Dei*. Since its formation in 2004, the Protestant Church in the Netherlands has sought to be a missionary church. For years the three denominations that merged in 2004 had been very much busy with the organization of the newly forming church. When the merger was completed there was a sense of urgency to focus more on the world outside the church. In *Kerk 2025* the church has stated that we have to accept the fact that there will not be in every village and suburb a church anymore. We have to accept 'open areas'. However, new congregations can still be formed. The PCN shows an increase in the number of temporary and part-time pastors, and of pioneers of would-be congregations. Also in established congregations the number of fulltime pastors has reduced rapidly. The ecclesial context is rapidly changing.

At the same time the church is re-organizing at the regional level. As noted above, the number of classis assemblies will be reduced from 76 to 11. These new classis assemblies will be about the size of the former provincial/particular synods. This will increase the geographical distance between the classis assembly and the local congregations. Of course, compared to the geographical distances within classis assemblies in North America or presbyteries in South Africa the distances are relative. Nevertheless, even with greater distances the classis assembly will still be the linchpin, the intermediate level linking the General Synod and the congregational consistories, and linking the consistories to the General Synod.

Kerk 2025 considers fellowship to be the main task of these new classis assemblies. The second task is supervision. These two aspects, while belonging to the nature of the classis assembly, focus on the inside of the ecclesial organization. Officially, this is in accord with the Reformed ecclesiology of the sixteenth century and the development of the classis assembly since the Synod of Emden of 1571. However, mission should be a (re)new(ed) aspect of the classis assembly, alongside supervision and fellowship (although the mission undertaken in this proposal will not necessarily have as its goal the formal establishment new congregations).

Missional ecclesiology requires new ecclesial language or at least transferring our 'old' ecclesial language into a new one, a new look at the church and church polity. This language is not (so much) about the structure, the functioning of the church, but about the essence and the nature of the church. This implies in our case also a missional classis assembly. So, not only a classis assembly that is about *episkopè* and *koinonia*, but also about being missional, because the classis assembly, as the intermediate level in a region between the consistories at the local level and the general synod at the national level, knows both worlds. Therefore, it can assist in supporting missional initiatives – local congregations or communities of believers, small or large, tenuous of solidly self-supporting. A classis assembly attuned to missional engagement will not only be occupied with and interested in internal ecclesial affairs, but will also be focused on the world beyond its present membership. From this perspective there is no need to ask whether the classis assembly has any function in tomorrow's church, or that it would better be abolished.

This is even more relevant as *Kerk 2025* speaks about the so-called *open areas*. One of the principles of *Kerk 2025* is that it is not necessary for the PCN to have a congregation in every village or city. The Protestant Church in the Netherlands accepts open areas: villages, cities, hamlets wherein there is no congregation. This matches the ecclesiastical situation in the Netherlands. It has become in many aspects a post-Christian country. This has consequences for the parochial or territorial system. The church has to accept these open areas, e.g. a territory where is no local PCN congregation with its consistory and a pastor or assistant-pastor. Although this might be considered sad news, it gives room for 'fresh expressions of church' (*Kerk 2025*, 10; *Church 2025*, 10.). These should not be burdened with current ecclesiastical customs, structures, and organization. In this way there is space to favor and stimulate new discoveries of being 'church'. Whenever a missionary pastor or assistant pastor is needed, he or she can be sent by the classis assembly (or by the classis pastor of this assembly) for the benefit of the missionary community.

This raises the question whether this is all the classis assembly can do, or whether the classis assembly can be more active as an expression of missional Reformed church polity. Someone or some board or organization or institute needs to be in charge of coordinating, guiding and stimulating fresh expressions of church. Among several protagonists, also the classis assembly can play a role, even in the new structure set forth in *Kerk 2025*. The Protestant Church in the Netherlands might want to include something like the Classis Renewal Ministry Team of the Christian Reformed Church in North America.

Classis Renewal Ministry Team

At the above-mentioned conference in New Brunswick NJ, USA I learned about contexts other than the Netherlands, and how those contexts shape classis assemblies – about differences, but also about resemblances. The Rev. Thea Lunk and the missiologist Craig van Gelder lectured about the Classis Renewal Ministry Team in the Christian Reformed Church. This team believes: "that classes are healthiest when they function as communities of fellowship, prayer, and spiritual growth; when they create and sustain healthy congregations; and when they facilitate shared ministry that is missional and transformational for individuals, neighborhoods and regions. With this in mind, the CRMT partners with classical leaders to pray, think, and plan how their classis can:

– work purposefully and creatively to be a healthy assembly of the church
– plan and participate in regional resource networks and other venues of collaboration
– encourage prayer, spiritual growth and faithful Christian living among leaders and congregations
– share learning, stories, and helpful practices
– connect pastoral and other congregational leaders with coaching and other resources
– advocate that the denomination's expectations for good order are fulfilled
– monitor benchmarks of classical vitality and take action as appropriate" (CR).

This team is concerned about the health of the classis assemblies. Its aim is to contribute to healthy assemblies. Also, this quote reveals that the classis assembly should facilitate shared ministry that is missional and transformational for persons, neighborhoods and regions. That implies that the classis assemblies, being missional in essence, do not necessarily need to undertake missionary tasks, but at least they can facilitate mission for the benefit of people, the church, the local and the regional society. This will contribute to the vitality of classis assemblies.

Again: Classis and Mission?

Concerning open areas at the local or regional level: because of the closure of church-buildings, the reduction in the number of congregations, the decline in the number of fulltime pastors, the merger of congregations, the lack of adequate membership to remain a vital congregation, the ecclesial map is already markedly changed and will soon change even more. This process has already started. The classis assembly can play a role in this context by supervising the regional ecclesial situation, facilitating pioneer or missional projects, or being proactive concerning such projects.

At present in the Protestant Church in the Netherlands it is not the classis assembly but the church at the national level which has responsibility for mission. However, I argue in this article that the classis assembly still can play an active role in missional work. It is (or should) not be a gathering or body only for internal affairs, but should be missional in its nature. Especially because the classis assembly knows the classis or region better than the national church. The PCN needs something like the Classis Renewal Ministry Team – not for internal affairs, but as a missional body, focused on the (external) context. However, there is more to be considered.

Paas has argued, in an article on government and leadership in mission "that there are three major difficulties with the Reformed ministry structure: (1) the lack of a consistent theology of the laity; (2) the lack of a supra-local ministry structure representing unity and mission; and, (3) the lack of movement and mobility created by an institutionalized church that is linked with a geographical parish system" (cf. Paas 2015, 116). I want to focus on the second point: the lack of a supra-local ministry structure representing unity and mission. The article concerns what type of government and/or leadership the fresh expressions of church need: "It may be worth considering a more complete pioneer ministry: ministers who have the authority to do itinerant work, going where they feel called to do mission, sent out by a local church, and supervised by a classis or synod, or perhaps a bishop. A missionary bishop could also be an important extension of the Reformed Word ministry. Such a model could stimulate the supra-local cause of mission and break through local stalemates" (cf. Paas 2015, 121).

Since the Synod of Emden of 1571, the presbyterial-synodical system of church governance obeys this golden rule: no congregation shall lord over another. However, obeying this rule has also its limits. The rule does not exclude good use of power, authority and governance. Paas states: "To avoid the abuse of power, we have often created a culture where nobody takes responsibility, where there is much investment in careful procedures and elaborate protocols, but where there are not fast and flexible responses to missionary opportunities. Why do we not consider the possibility that the abuse of power is not primarily caused by a failing control system but by spiritual failure? A healthy ministry structure is not primarily fostered by checks and balances but by a healthy spirituality that is rooted in a clear theology of the offices" (Paas 2015, 124). From a judicial perspective and the angle of seeking for justice it is good that there is a system of checks and balances. Even in a missional context. However, this does not exclude (and here I agree with Paas) "[a] supra-local office, a bishop, with a specific but limited task of guarding and stimulating the church's mission, and with the authority to override the decisions of local church councils in the interest of mission" (Paas 2015, 124).

The Reformed system of church governance already has such a bishop: the classis assembly. It is an expression of the collegial type of supervision (*episkope*), not a personal type of supervision. It is an expression of the catholicity of the church. Of course, the local church is quite important, but there is more than just the local churches. They can be too busy with their own internal affairs. In the words of Paas: "The authority of a bishop, or a superintendent, overseeing a city or a region with several parishes, could be a great help against local church councils that jealously guard their turf" (Paas 2015, 115). The classis assembly as the missional bishop helps to avoid the decoy of the emphasis on the local church and taking care of only the internal affairs and members. According to Lesslie Newbigin, instead of focusing on one's own denomination or own church and internal structure "churches should instead send their best people, and especially their ministers, to those areas where the church is under pressure and where it is bleeding members. This is what leadership in mission means. Clearly, this is not the natural reflex of our churches, nor is it the way we look at our church offices" (Paas 2015, 112, quoting Newbigin 1889, 235f.).

Mission or church planting should not be focused on establishing new local churches according to the tradition, in order to fulfil the empty places in the Reformed map of the Netherlands. Mission history shows that many of these initially fresh congregations later became too vulnerable and had to be dissolved. Church planting gives space to fresh expressions of church, not necessarily to establishing churches. Local churches in a certain district should need each other and join forces, and make use of a missional bishop, either the classis assembly as an expression of a missional church or a missional bishop, as an elaboration of the role of the classis pastor. This classis pastor is to be a pastoral assignment. It is to include 'edifying the ecclesiastical life and the missional presentation of the church in the region'. The tasks of the classis pastor of the new classis "include building the ecclesiastical life and establishing a missionary presence for the church in the region" (Kerk 2025 21f., cf. Church 2025, 21:). The latter part needs to be clarified and elaborated in *Kerk 2025* and its implementation by the General Synod of the PCN.

The classis pastor of the new classis assembly in *Kerk 2025* should not only be a helpdesk for local churches and its consistories, and for edifying the faithful, but also have an external perspective, creating space for and supporting fresh expressions of church, urban or rural, as new forms of monastic or university communities, in houses or at schools, at factories or in hospitals. And, of course, when possible even newly established congregations, with the offices of deacon, elders and pastor. Again Paas, commenting on research by Martijn Vellekoop: "There is simply a lot of church planting that amounts to denominational expansion, disguised as mission" (Paas 2012, 474, note 28). Paas goes on to say: " Some denominations ... still legitimate their church planting activities on their websites with phrases like this: 'We plant churches, because our denomination is still absent in many places.' This pertains to mere denominational expansion, and it deserves every criticism that has been leveled against it, for example by Roman Catholics and Ecumenical Protestants. We do not need more churches, but we desperately need contextual and credible churches. As far as this is more a matter of innovation than adaptation I think we cannot and should not avoid new church planting. More than ever before we need incubators of creativity, sacrifice, and inspiration at the organizational margins of ecclesiastical life. This, and nothing else, legitimates church planting in a post-Christian society" (Paas 2012, 474f.).

Kerk 2025, as stated, acknowledges the fact that there are and will be more empty spaces in the Netherlands. The Protestant Church in the Netherlands should not try to fill the empty spaces with traditional churches. That is not missional. Being missional is trying something new without knowing the outcome, on the basis of the Gospel.

Also, *Kerk 2025* gives room to a kind of a supra-local officer. It is not a bishop, nor a superintendent. The name of this officer is 'classis pastor'. This officer does have some power. To grant authority to such a supra-local officer is a new thing for Dutch Reformed church polity. This officer is to be involved in the supervision and fellowship of the congregations and consistories in the region or classis, in short: for internal ecclesial affairs. When the classis has a history of mission, of giving space to and providing a framework for fresh expressions of church, why should this not be an opportunity for today and the future? The classis infrastructure not only requires a revision as in *Kerk 2025*, but also in really being and/or becoming a missional church – one that is not only occupied with establishing congregations as the main goal of its missional work, but creating and safeguarding a framework for fresh expressions of church.

Conclusions

As the church is missional in its nature, so the classis assembly should be missional in its nature and reality. This includes giving space to church planting alongside establishing or reorganizing local churches. The classis assembly, as the missional Reformed type of *episcope*, is not only concerned with its own ecclesiastical business. Of course, there is nothing wrong with good internal governance and structure, not at all. It does matter. However, missional church polity will make space for fresh expressions of church. Church planting implies church renewal. A missional church is aware of that. A missional bishop, whether in the form of an assembly or a single office-bearer, or a combination of both, can assist the local churches in developing awareness of the connection between mission and renewal, in order that the church can flourish.

Abbreviations and bibliography

ACTA 1985: Acta van het Synodaal Convent (1887) en van de voorlopige synoden van de Nederduitsche Gereformeerde Kerken (1888–1892). Kampen: Kok, 1985, 584–99.

CR: Christian Reformed Church in North America. Classis Resources. Accessed February 1, 2018. https://www.crcna.org/resources/other-resources/classis-resources.

CRMT: Classis Renewal Ministry Team

PCN: Protestant Church in the Netherlands

GP 1992: Gemeenten en predikanten van de Gereformeerde Kerken in Nederland: Publikatie ter gelegenheid van 100 jaar Gereformeerde Kerken in Nederland 17 juni 1992, Algemeen secretariaat van de Gereformeerde Kerken in Nederland (ed.). Leusden, 1992.

VOC: The United East Indies Company

WIC: The West Indies Company Janssen, Allan J., and Leo J. Koffeman (eds.). 2014. Protestant Church Polity in Changing Contexts I: Ecclesiological and Historical Contributions. Proceedings of the International Conference, Utrecht, The Netherlands, 7–10 November, 2011. Series: Church Polity and Ecumenism: Global Perspectives 2. Zurich/Berlin: LIT Verlag.

Janssen, Allan J., and Leon van den Broeke (eds.). 2010. The Collegial Bishop: Classis and Presbytery at Issue. Series: The Historical Series of the Reformed Church of America 66. Grand Rapids MI: Eerdmans.

Kerk 2025: Waar een Woord is, is een weg. Accessed February 1, 2018. https://www.protestantsekerk.nl/Kerk2025/Kerk2025. English translation: Church 2025: Where there's a Word, there's a way. https://www.protestantsekerk.nl/download/CAwdEAwUUkBLVg$==$&inline$=$0.

Luttikhuis, Bernard A.M. 1992. Een grensgeval: Oorsprong en functie van het territoriale beginsel in het gereformeerde kerkrecht. Gorinchem: Narratio.

Newbigin, Lesslie. 1989. The Gospel in a Pluralist Society. Grand Rapids: Eerdmans.

Niemandt, Nelus. 2014. Emerging Missional Ecclesiology in the Dutch Reformed Church in South Africa and Church Polity. In: Janssen and Koffeman 2014, 65–81.

Paas, Stefan. 2012. Church Renewal by Church Planting: The Significance of Church Planting for the Future of Christianity in Europe. In: Theology Today 68/4 (2011), 1–11

Paas, Stefan. 2015. Leadership in Mission: The Reformed System of Church Governance in an Age of Mission. In: Calvin Theological Journal 50/1 (2015), 106–121.

Rutgers, Frederik L. (ed.). 1899. Acta van de Nederlandsche synoden der zestiende eeuw. 's Gravenhage: Martinus Nijhoff. [Reprint Dordrecht: J.P. van den Tol, 1980, 2nd. Ed.]

Van den Broeke, Leon. 2010. Classis in crisis: Om de classicale toekomst. Zoetermeer: Boekencentrum.

Van den Broeke, C. [Leon]. 2005. Een geschiedenis van de classis: Classicale typen tussen idee en werkelijkheid 1571–2004. Kampen: Kok.

Van den Broeke, C. [Leon]. 2011. Bishop-in-presbytery: De classicale bisschop? In: NTKR: Tijdschrift voor Recht en Religie 5 (2011), 140–62.

THE HINDRANCES OF DENOMINATIONAL CHURCH ORDER TO CHURCH UNITY

Leepo Modise and Basimane Makoko

DRC FAMILY IN SOUTH AFRICA 1971–2015

Introduction

Church unity is the Biblical imperative for all church members despite their circumstances. Church unity is not a question of choice – the people of God are sure that it is God's will according to his Word. One should distinguish between church unity and the unification of the church. Church unity is a gift, the unification of the church, or rather of churches, is something the people of God should work towards achieving. In this paper, the focus will be on church unification (the process), this process need to be guided by the church order and regulations of the involved denominations. Firstly, we will handle the identity of denominations studied in this research study, namely: Dutch Reformed Church (DRC), Uniting Reformed Church in Southern Africa (URCSA), Reformed Church in Africa (RCA) and the Former Dutch Reformed Church in Africa (DRCA). Secondly, the confessional basis article of the church order of these denominations will be highlighted and discussed in relation to its hindrance to Church unity. Its article on a confessional basis will be investigated in terms of its closeness or openness for further confessing if need be. Thirdly, the adoption process of the Belhar Confession and its impact on church unity, with special references to the church order, will be discussed. Finally, how can a provisional church order assist the main role players to grow, work and live towards church unity?

Aims of the study

The main aim of this research study is to respond to the question: do denominational church orders or polities foster or hinder unity between and among churches? This main aim is sub-divided into three specific aims. The first is to describe the identification of the role players in church unification from within their church order. Secondly, to illustrate how URCSA and the other three role players differ in terms of their confessional basis and the openness as well as closeness to the acceptance of new confessions. Thirdly, to demonstrate how church orders of DRCA and DRC were and are a hindrance to church unification.

The identity of main role players in drc-urcsa family unity talks

It will assist the readers of this contribution to have a clear picture who are the role players in this section. We will clarify the role players in terms of the apartheid classification of people in South Africa even though apartheid is no more there, but its legacy still exists in these denominations. URCSA is a denomination formed by the former DRCA of predominantly blacks and the Dutch Reformed Mission Church (DRMC) which consisted predominantly of colored people; these churches united on the 14th of April, 1994. The DRC is a denomination of the whites only. The RCA predominantly consists of Indians, while the present DRCA still is a church for black people. This classification will assist in terms of what kind of unity is needed, whether racial or denominational unity. The identities of these role players will be discussed in the following paragraphs.

The identity of the four main role players in the unification process has been provided by the delegates of these denominations at the Volmoed meeting on the 13 – 15 July 2015. The meeting in Volmoed was intended to discuss the way forward after the DRC had failed to obtain a one hundred percent 'yes' vote from their ten regional synods. The information about these identities is captured in the 'Volmoed report', the (so far unpublished) report of this meeting and the decisions taken by the group from the DRC, the URCSA, the DRCA and the RCA that met at Volmoed. The following was reported as the identity of individual denominations.

The DRC identifies itself as a Reformed and missional church. The denomination has seen a shift towards becoming a missional church as a major policy shift. According to the report, the following is stated:

- A totally diverse church with a broad spectrum of modalities in the structure and function of their congregations, their worship styles and in the functioning of the Presbyteries.
- Congregations have changed their attitude towards traditional concepts of pastoral home visitation and broader pastoral care.
- A denomination that places great emphasis on theological training both in terms of the effort of ensuring that people are trained correctly and in budgeting to make sure that this happens.

- The language of worship remains important; while other languages may be used, Afrikaans is still important.
- They are, at the same time both extremely Reformed and extremely evangelical and these two values are seen as very important.
- An African church that sees itself in Southern Africa to stay and that is committed to Africa (Volmoed Report, 2015).

The DRCA identifies itself as a black and Reformed church. This is stated in the report by the DRCA: the denomination felt that it was very important that in the process of unification, each denomination should retain its own structure up to synodical level, that unification should not destroy or swallow the DRCA. Their desire was that unity should positively impact the ministry of all members, and they were thinking particularly of the ministry of elders who played an important role in their congregations (Volmoed Report, 2015).

The following points were highlighted as the identity of DRCA:
- They are Reformed in tradition.
- They are a black church in terms of the color of the skin.
- They value Ubuntu.
- They identify the need to direct their activities outwards, the development of an external focus, a missional focus in which they emphasize the need to reach out with the gospel.
- They identify their ecumenical spirit in the shared life of the communities in which they were present, where people would join with others at funerals and worship would often be shared among congregations of various denominations (Volmoed Report, 2015).

The URCSA identifies itself as an African and Reformed church. According to the report the following aspects characterize the identity of URCSA:
- The denomination sees itself as the Church of the Belhar Confession.
- They are a Reformed church in Africa, by which they mean that they are a denomination in which Scripture and Confession continually inform their church life.
- Being African, Ubuntu in the sense of mutual responsibility together with love and care for each other is emphasized. In addition, their African identity is demonstrated in a commitment to Ujamaa, which they defined as togetherness embedded in their church order (e.g. co-urcsa, art 4.3, 4.4, cf. Belhar Confession, art. 4: the need to minister to people on the margins).
- They see themselves as a confessing denomination that is both united and uniting.
- They are an ecumenical denomination that is trans-cultural. In their denomination, one culture does not dominate another, but it is affirming of all cultures. They have adopted an open system of symbols with other cultures; they encour-

age individuals to embrace the many cultures represented in the denomination and they are multi-lingual.
- They have a strong prophetic ministry which is manifested in a critique of the status quo coming from the 80's and 90's and continuing to the present day (Volmoed Report, 2015).

The RCA identifies itself as a small church, but not insignificant even in the Indian community. According to the report the following aspects regard the identity of RCA:

- Liturgically, their worship style is a participatory worship; because people were looking for a more expressive style of worship, many had left their denomination to join the Pentecostal and Charismatic churches.
- They are a missional church in that they are committed to spreading the gospel.
- They are a Reformed denomination.
- The Word of God is primary and the Confessions play a vital role.
- In 1990 the denomination produced the Laudium Declaration, which was modelled after the Barmen Declaration.
- The RCA is defined as an evangelical church with the challenge and task to reach people of Asian descent, especially people from Hindu and Muslim backgrounds.
- The denomination is a conservative church.
- Most of the congregations are predominantly Indian and this affects the questions of denominational identity (Volmoed Report, 2015).

The above points were highlighted in this important meeting of the four role players on the unity talks of the DRC-URCSA family. It is very important to note from the above that most of the people who were presenting the identity of the different denominations have put more emphasis on the practical and contextual issues and very little on the church order. These practical and contextual issues have their own contribution to the challenge to church unity within the DRC family and URCSA, but the key hindrance lies in the church order articles. For the purpose of this section we will focus on the URCSA and DRC, and particularly on article 1 of both churches in their church order. Vorster rightly indicates that, in order to understand the concept church order, one needs to pay attention to the principles that are expressed in article 1 of the church order of the Reformed Churches of South Africa (see Vorster 1999, 13). Throughout the Reformed tradition this article has been the foundation of Reformed Church polity. Article 1 of both the DRC and the URCSA emphasizes the identity of such churches. In the URCSA article 1, the emphasis is on the church as communion of believers in Christ called by the Holy Spirit to be a nation of God, while the DRC is more on the doctrine of the church, the Bible as the infallible Word of God, and the confessional basis. Moving from article 1 of URCSA one might identify URCSA as God-people centered church, this is supported by article 4 of the Belhar Confession, which states that God stands on the side of the marginalized and the church should stand where God stands (Belhar Confession, 1986). In contrast, the DRC is doctrinal in its nature, hence its article one emphasis doctrines. URCSA being a God-people centered church, it is very easy for it to be an open church for unity with its unity friendly church order.

The church orderly way of adopting the Belhar Confession by the DRC family

The argument for accepting the Belhar Confession in a church orderly way has a history as far back as 1990, in the former Dutch Reformed Church in Africa (DRCA) during the extra-ordinary General synod sitting in Cape Town, October 1990. The issue on the table of the synod of 1990 was the unification of the two daughter churches of the DRC, namely the DRCA and the DRMC. The synod started its discussion from the declaration of DRCA and DRMC which was drafted by the *Gesprekskommissie* (discussion commission). There was a notion that the two denominations must unite to become one church. Furthermore, the two denominations had committed themselves to the unification process to be one church (Ligstraal 1990). The church order challenge to the DRCA came to surface when acceptance of the Belhar Confession was introduced to the synod. The General Synod delegates voted in majority in favor of the acceptance of the Belhar Confession. The church orderly question was raised in that meeting relating to CO-DRCA, article 36.1, which orders the regional synods to vote also in favor of inclusion of the Belhar Confession as the fourth confession of DRCA. The question was, is it still necessary that regional synods must approve the confession as article 36.1 determines the church to follow. The then DRCA saw article 36.1 to be an obstacle to church unity in terms of the Belhar Confession. The Synod decided to remove the obstacle by deleting article 36.1 in order to pave the way to church unity. According to Ligstraal: "At this synod a decision was taken to delete article 36.1, the synod thought that, by deleting this article it has cleared church polity problem out of the way. It was no longer necessary for the regional synods to approve the Belhar Confession" (Ligstraal 1990, 1; transl. by the authors).

Some of the delegates were not satisfied with the way the synod had handled the amendment of the church order, the reason being that the amendment of the church order was never an item in the agenda of the synod, and there were no recommendations of the permanent judicial commission. They based their argument on the regulation of order 2.3 on how matters are brought before the synod. Regulation of order 2.3 of the former DRCA determines that a matter to the agenda of the synod should reach the scribe of the Synod three months before the meeting, in order to be referred to the relevant commission, which will introduce the matter to the synod with recommendations to the meeting. In this regard, this church orderly way was not followed; the meeting saw it differently as the obstacle to church unity, then the synod did everything beyond its power to pave the way to church unity (Ligstraal, November 1990). In this regard, the church orderly way was not followed, but the matter was tabled and dealt with in the meeting. The votes were as follows 58 voters for the amendment and 38 voters against the amendment. This result led the opponents of the amendment to take the argument further to article 36.2.

Furthermore, this matter led the synod to bypass or limit article 36.2, which states that the amendment of the church order should be approved by two-third majority of the synod. The question was, are the voters for the amendment two-third majority of the synod? In this regard, the synod has accepted the Belhar Confession and the spirit of the Belhar Confession has moved the synod beyond the church order imperative. This spirit is embedded in article 3 of the Belhar Confession, that says that church unity is a gift from God and the people of God need to strive for church unity, despite all the law ad rule of this world. Throughout history in South Africa, the acceptance of the Belhar Confession has been a challenge to church unity.

The inter-relatedness of confession and church order is indeed typical of Reformed theology. Distinctive of the Reformation of the Church during the 16th century was that only Scripture truth should be obeyed and received. This was formulated as *sola Scriptura*. This simply means that the authority of the church should be carried by the Word of God. This represents the starting line of Reformed thinking on what the church should be and how the church should be governed and ordered (Jonker 1965, 17).

Plomp argues that the term 'Reformed' does not imply immobility or use of the same practical measures over and over again (see Plomp 1992, 38–40). An important insight in the Reformed environment is that a genuine Reformed church polity serves and by so doing assists churches to be governed by the Word of God. A true Reformed church polity is by no means an end in itself, but serves to keep Christ and the Word at the head of the church. Some scholars even call it a serving justice. Strauss supports the argument of Plomp that a church polity and a church order are not meant to provide laws that should be strictly followed or go into a dot and point of church life (see Strauss 2010, 1ff.). It should rather provide orderly channels through which the Word can flow freely to determine the ordering of church businesses. The implication is that a Reformed church polity is adaptable to new circumstances and keeps its identity as a polity serving the Word of God in the process.

The in-depth interpretation of the notion of Plomp and Strauss will be understood as justification of the action of the former DRCA in 1990. The church order, according to these church polity scholars, paves the way for the application of the Word of God. In this instance, church unity as a gift and a biblical imperative weigh more than the church order directives. The suspension of article 36.2 of the church order was just but a means to allow the free flow of the Word of God leading to church unification. Makoko indicates that in 1618 the Synod of Dordt adopted a church order that complied with the following sequence: The Bible, confession and church order, which means that the Word of God determined what the church had to say and then, the conviction of church on that and then the order or regulations of the church (see Makoko 2010, 9).

Furthermore, CO-DRCA, art. 36.1 seems to be a hindrance to the church unity between DRCA and DRMC. In the same breath the general synod of 1990, that had taken a brave stance against its own church orderly process, experienced another obstacle from the DRMC in the form of a letter. This letter raises the concern about the church orderly procedures followed by the DRCA to amend its article 36.1. The letter suggests the delay of the unification process, until the DRCA would follow the correct church order procedures. Dr Sam Buti, chair of the DRCA general synod, clarified that article 36.1 was no more an obstacle to church unification; this clarification would then allow the DRMC to continue with unification with immediate effect. The argument above indicates that church order articles are in most cases hindrances to church unification.

Modise states that there was hope from the side of URCSA after the decision of the General Synod of DRC 2011, that the synod starts the process to accept the Belhar Confession at the General synod level (see Modise 2016). Furthermore, the General Synod would facilitate the process down to congregations, presbyteries and regional synods. This process was seen as a massive breakthrough in the DRC, but at the same time there was a stumbling block that was standing ahead of the process of accepting the Belhar Confession and its inclusion in art. 1 of the CO-DRC. One needs to remember the importance of the Belhar Confession to URCSA as the main identity of this church: the acceptance of the Belhar Confession means a breakthrough in the unification process.

The church order articles now become a hindrance to the acceptance and inclusion of the Belhar Confession in the CO-DRC, which consequently becomes a hindrance to the unification process. The stumbling block is CO-DRC art. 44, which states:

> 44.1 Amendment of the Confession is possible only after it has been approved by a two-thirds majority of each synod and two-thirds of all the church councils, each supporting it with a two-thirds majority.

44.2 Article 44.1 and 44.2 of the Church Order are amended after each synod has approved it with a two-thirds majority and General Synod thereafter approves it with a two-thirds majority.

44.3 General Synod may, with the exception of article 44.1 and 44.2, amend or augment the Church Order with a two-thirds majority.

This means that all regional synods should obtain a two-third majority for this church order article to be changed. In the process of accepting the Belhar Confession, seven out of ten regional synods could not reach the two-third majority that is required by the church order articles, while only three regional synods could reach the two-third majority. Taking these statistics and article 44.1 of the DRC into consideration, it stands to reason that the Belhar Confession cannot be included in the confessional basis of the DRC, in Article 1 (see Modise 2016).

Furthermore, Modise postulates that the CO-DRC is formulated in a manner that church unity in relation to the Belhar Confession should be very tricky. One needs to look how the DRC plays with words within article 44 in terms of the amendments of article 44.1 and 44.2: all other articles can be amended by a two-third majority of the General Synod, while 44.1 and 44.2 can only be amended after all regional synods have first approved it with two-third majority, and then the General synod with two-third majority. It becomes clear that DRC or its church polity experts have formulated CO-DRC, art. 44, to become a gatekeeper for the Belhar Confession not to be included in its church order (see Modise 2016). It is the lesson that the people of South Africa have learned from the apartheid era that if one needs to keep people separate one needs to have many acts and regulations, this is the same situation in the DRC at this point in time. The church order articles have played a major role in the church orderly process to accept the Belhar Confession and not to include it in CO-DRC, art. 1.

If the church order articles exclude the Belhar Confession from being part of the four role players' church orders, therefore the church orders of the four role players are a hindrance to the unification process. The main reason is that the Belhar Confession is part of the package of the church unification process, together with church unity and restorative justice. If one may use the metaphor of the three-legged pot for the united church within the DRC-URCSA family perspective, without the Belhar Confession this united church will not stand. These three points are the points of reference in the Memorandum of Agreement between URCSA and DRC (MOU 2011; cf. Modise, 2016).

The parallel growth with the provisional order in between to enhance trust and relationship

The failure of the DRC to obtain a two-third majority from ten regional synods was a blow to URCSA that could have caused the URCSA to stage a walk out of re-unification talks. The URCSA leadership felt that walking out would contradict the functionality of the Belhar Confession. The spirit of Belhar Confession kept the leadership of URCSA around the table for only one reason: Belhar is the identity of URCSA and members need to live it out in all spheres of life. The executive of URCSA listens to its confession and stays on negotiations because they confess that church unity is a gift and on the other hand an obligation that the people of God need to strive for. In that spirit the DRC family and URCSA in their meeting in 25–26 May 2015 decided to take another turn, where they decided on a Provisional Church Order (PCO) that will create a room for congregations, presbyteries and regional synods from the DRC family to start from the ground to work together towards church unity. The other turn was the permission of the DRC General Synod of 2015 that has given a regional synod who had accepted the Belhar Confession permission to include it in its regional church order. We would like to quote the Preamble and the statement of intent of the Provisional Church Order:

> We as the four churches have decided to journey together called by the Triune God to participate in His mission to the world, so that the world may believe that God has sent Jesus as Savior to the world.
>
> We, therefore, envisage a new reunited church in the DRC Family, which is missional, committed to the Biblical demands of love, reconciliation, justice and peace.
>
> We realize this process will present many challenges and issues to contend with, but we accept the challenges in being obedient to our Lord and His Word.
>
> We are called to a life, ministry and ecclesiology of obedience and sacrifice.
>
> Knowing that walking this road will ask us to put all selfish ambition aside and to give ourselves as Christ did, we do this in active response to the gospel that Christ in His mercy poured out on us. We respond to Christ's love and Spirit who unites us to Christ in a deep and eternal fellowship. We acknowledge that Christ already gained the victory over all opposing forces so that we can look forward in hope to that day when all knees shall bow and every tongue confess that Jesus Christ is Lord (Phil 1:27 – 2:18).
>
> We are committed to accept all the gifts brought by the four churches to the reconciliation, restoration and reunification process (PCO, Preamble).

However, there is another way of looking at it. If church unity is a given, a fruit of the redemption wrought on the cross, is it not true that the people of God should accept one another unconditionally? Is this not what God does, not justifying the righteous, but the godless? Is agreement on the articles of faith or cross of Christ the basis for unity? Should churches (re-)unite because they agree with each other or should they (re-)unite because they are one in Christ, and afterwards grow closer to each other in their faith while they live in mutual fellowship? What is the best situation for agreement: living at a distance and bargaining in a negotiation process, or living in fellowship in which we share something of our life experience? Is not one of the grave problems of the DRC from grassroots up to the level of the local church council and minister that these whites have had virtually no exposure to the atrocities of the apartheid era – in state, society and church – and that the only hope of their ever having such exposure may be in living in the same local church as those Christians who have experienced apartheid directly? Does not the name Uniting Reformed Church invite this church to go into a unification process with the DRC without the condition of prior acceptance of the Belhar Confession (see Modise, 2016)?

The Provisional Church Order will be an avenue that will allow the four churches to grow together and to know each other better like the first church of Acts 2:42–47. The Provisional Church Order and the Memorandum of Agreement provide a safe space to grow together closer to each other without acceptance of the Belhar Confession, but living the Belhar Confession by standing where God stands on the side of the poor. These churches that are growing towards being one should bear in mind that the Memorandum of Agreement states that the Belhar Confession will be the confession of the new united church (cf. MOU 2011, 4.1).

Conclusion

In conclusion, whenever one uses the church order articles one needs to consider the Word of God, the confession, the tradition and the context where the article is applied. The church order articles (article 1) of the church order of the other three role players in the unification process of the DRC family are closed ended, confessing only the three classical Reformed confessions, while article 2 of the church order of the Uniting Reformed Church in Southern Africa is open ended in this wording: "The Uniting Reformed Church in Southern Africa accepts that it has not completed its task of confessing the faith. Changed circumstances and a better understanding of God's Word in the future may lead to the acceptance of further articles of faith, or the revision of the existing articles of faith" (CO-URCSA, art. 2.3).

Abbreviations and bibliography

CO-DRC: Church Order of the Dutch Reformed Church (2011)
CO-DRCA: Church Order of the Dutch Reformed Church in Africa

CO-URCSA: Church Order of the Uniting Reformed Church in Southern Africa
DRC: Dutch Reformed Church
DRCA: Dutch Reformed Church in Africa
DRMC: Dutch Reformed Mission Church
MOU: Memorandum of Agreement between URCSA and DRC of 2011. Accessed January 29, 2018. http://www.ngkerkas.co.za/wp-content/uploads/2013/04/textsc{urcsa-drc}.pdf.
PCO: Provisional Order with respect to the re-unification of churches within the Dutch Reformed church family. Accessed January 29, 2018. http://urcsa.net/documents
RCA: Reformed Church in Africa
URCSA: Uniting Reformed Church in Southern Africa

Jonker, Willem D. 1965. Die Aard van die Kerklike Gesag. In: Die Kerkbode, 8 December 1965.
Ligstraal, Official News Bulletin of the DRCA, November 1990, Number 11.
Makoko, Basimane P. 2010. The correlation between the Confession of Belhar and the Church Order of the Uniting Reformed Church in Southern Africa: An overview. Bloemfontein: University of Free State (Masters of Arts).
Modise, Leepo J. 2016. The unification process in the Dutch Reformed Church (DRC) family and Uniting Reformed Church in Southern Africa (URCSA): The confessional basis and Confession of Belhar. *Studia Historiae Ecclesiasticae,* 39(1), 185–203.
Plomp, Jan. 1992. Kerk en recht. In: Van't Spijker and Van Drimmelen 1992, 32–42.
Strauss, Piet J. 2010. *Kerk en orde vandag.* Bloemfontein: Sunmedia.
Van't Spijker, Willem and Van Drimmelen, Leen C. (eds.). Inleiding tot de studie van het kerkrecht. Kampen: Kok.
Volmoed Report 2015 (unpublished).
Vorster, JM. 1999. An introduction to Reformed Church Polity. Noordbrug: Potchefstroom Theological Publications.

MISSION AND CHURCH POLITY IN THE DUTCH REFORMED CHURCH OF SOUTH AFRICA

CJP (Nelus) Niemandt

Introduction

The Dutch Reformed Church in South Africa (DRC) adopted a new policy on the missional nature and calling of the DRC in 2013: *Raamwerkdokument oor die missionale aard en roeping van die NG Kerk* [Framework document on the missional nature and calling of the DRC] (NG Kerk 2013a, 199–215). The new policy document was described as an expression of discernment processes on the essence and nature of the church and its witness in the world, covering more than a decade of discussions, decisions, and developments in the DRC. The goal of the policy document was described as the creation of new missional language that may ignite a new missional imagination for the DRC.

The process that led to the adoption of the framework document were described in two earlier case studies on the missional development of the DRC (see Niemandt 2015a; Niemandt 2014). This paper builds on those case studies and tracks the missional transformation of the DRC, specifically in terms of church polity and church order, after the 2013 General Synod.

The 2015 General Synod received five reports on matters related to the missional transformation of the denomination, covering the following areas: Liturgy and missional church (NG Kerk 2015a, 114–121); congregational development (NG Kerk 2015a, 122–124); equipping church members (NG Kerk 2015a, 125–127); missional ecclesiology (NG Kerk 2015a, 128–132); as well as a joint report by all the task teams doing work related to missional ecclesiology (NG Kerk 2015a, 138–143). The number of reports and the wide-ranging issues addressed in these reports serve as an indication of the intense focus of the General Synod on missional ecclesiology.

The executive of the DRC decided, at the very first meeting of their term, to prioritize the continued missional transformation of the DRC as its most important strategic goal (NG Kerk 2015b, 14). It also decided to prioritize a revision of the church order of the DRC, in order to align the church order with the policy decisions made by the General Synod (NG Kerk 2015a, 240). The chairperson of the executive, Nelis Janse van Rensburg, promised a new 'missional church order' in an opinion piece in the official mouthpiece of the DRC (see Janse van Rensburg 2016).

Another important factor plays into this revision of the DRC church order – unity talks between the four churches comprising the Dutch Reformed family of churches – i.e. the DRC, the Uniting Reformed Church in Southern Africa (urcsa), the Reformed Church in Africa (RCA), as well as the Dutch Reformed Church in Africa (DRCA) – progressed to the point where the four churches decided to enter into a process to develop an interim church order for a united church (NG Kerk 2015c, 15). This interim church order opens up exciting possibilities in terms of the identity and witness of the DRC, and any discussion on church polity and missional identity needs to take cognizance of these developments. The interim order, for example, states the following on the missional identity of the proposed new united church:

> We as the four churches have decided to journey together, called by the Triune God to participate in His mission to the world, so that the world may believe that God has sent Jesus as Savior to the world.
>
> We therefore, envisage a new reunited church in the DRC Family, which is missional, committed to the Biblical demands of love, reconciliation, justice and peace (NG Kerk 2015a, 240).

The Executive of the DRC also decided to study the possibilities of compiling a contemporary missional approach to unity in the denomination and DRC-family of churches (NG Kerk 2015b, 12). The scope of this paper does not allow a wider discussion of this issue, but it certainly constitutes a major element of future developments.

1. Church polity and the strengthening of the church's missional identity

It is against this background that questions regarding the relationship between a missional policy and church polity arises. How can church polity and order undergird and strengthen the DRC's newfound missional identity?

1.1. The role of a church order in the drc

The first issue is a brief overview of the role and influence of the church order in the DRC. Church polity serves the church and must reflect the identity, calling, life, and order of the church. It is the architecture of the life of the church (Dingemans

1987, 9). Church polity reflects a theological position on ecclesiology (Koffeman 2009, 11–13). Strauss says: "The church order describes the identity and deepest beliefs of a denomination" (see Strauss 2013, 20).

This is clearly the case in the life and praxis of the DRC. The church order does not only reflect a theological position in the sense that it is an expression of policy, but it also informs and forms church praxis. This is evident from the explanation found in the DRC church order. The very first section discusses the confessions, identity, and order of the church, and article 3 states:

> 3.1 Whereas the Word of God requires that everything in the congregation of Christ should proceed in a proper and orderly manner (1 Corinthians 14:40), a number of regulations are given in the following articles for the life and work of the Church with a view to the fulfilment of its task and calling in accordance with Holy Scriptures and the Confession.
>
> 3.2 These regulations deal with the offices in the Church, the assemblies of the Church, the work of the Church, governance and discipline of the Church, and the external relationships of the Church (NG Kerk 2013b, 1).

Note the formulation that the regulations are given for 'the life and work of the Church' and that the regulations deal with 'the work of the Church'. This is clearly the conventional understanding in the denomination. This can be explained in a striking example – Strauss refers to decisions of the DRC executive that interprets the unity in the denomination as unity in the Word and confession, and he draws particular attention to the fact that the executive understands this to mean that unity finds expression in one church order (see Strauss 2013, 21).

My conclusion is that the church order plays a defining role in the life and praxis of the DRC. It gives expression to the identity of the denomination and regulates church life and praxis. This is also evident in the way the church order has been used to stop significant changes in the policy of the DRC regarding same-sex relationships and marriages. More than 21 appeals, based on interpretations of the church order, have been lodged against decisions of the General Synod in 2015 (see Jackson 2016).

1.2. The power relations behind the understanding of the importance of church order in the drc, especially the influence of actuarii in the drc

The church order is not a sterile document, but it determines power and power relations in the DRC. Texts, especially institutionalized texts or discourses such as church orders, constitute church practice. We do things through words. Words are a form of action (see Fairclough 1992, 71). Not only are texts produced and consumed but also distributed in specific genres and in particular contexts which all have an influence on the way meaning is constructed and participants positioned in certain roles (see Fairclough 1992, 126). Fairclough argues that there is a close relationship between language and power, and that sociolinguistic conventions arise out of and give rise to particular relations of power (see Fairclough 2013, 1).

One of the more important institutionalized power relations in the DRC is found in the *Algemene Steunspan Regte* [General Synod Support team: Polity]. This team is formed by the *actuarii* of the participating synods, the *actuarius* of the General Synod, the lecturers teaching church polity, and other technical advisors. Many regional synods also have one or other form of such a structure. This team advises the General Synod on the 'interpretation and application' of the church order (NG Kerk 2013b, 33). Regional synods are advised by regional teams. In practical terms, this means that the real levers of power and influence in the denomination resides in these task teams. The practice in the DRC is that individuals, congregations, and other structures can approach the relevant *actuarii* for advice on the interpretation of the church order. My observation is that this (mostly written) advice does play a very important role in the way in which the church order is applied, and thus affects church praxis.

The life and actions of a complex system such as a denomination, and the flow of change, are influenced by the relationship between 'traders' and 'gatekeepers' in the system. Traders are at the forefront of change. They are the 'innovators' and 'early adopters' in the system (Keifert 2006, 55). Traders ring in changes and introduce new grammar, ideas, and innovations. Gatekeepers see themselves as custodians of the past and the traditions in the system. They guard the identity of the system. In my opinion, teams that are tasked with the interpretation and application of the church order of a denomination will attract more gatekeepers than traders, and such teams are naturally inclined to see their role as custodians of the tradition and identity, rather than agents of change. This opens the way for using the church order to control the flow of transformation and change in the system. The fact that *actuarii* and church order task teams can give substantial guidance on the 'interpretation and application' of the church order, combined with the fact that there is no formal review of guidance by *actuarii*, grants exceptional structural powers to *actuarii*, stymies creative adaptive changes, and eventually the missional character of the church. Fairclough refers to the power of the written language. It is a one-sided discourse, with a sharp divide between producers and interpreters (see Fairclough 2013, 41).

Missional theology is about the core identity of the church. A choice for a missional ecclesiology changes everything – first and foremost the church order. Roxburgh argues that denominations face critical choices – to either remain inside the city gates (gatekeepers) or to risk the liminal experiences that lie outside the walls (traders). To risk it outside the gates involves the grammar of an organizational self-understanding centered on the participation in God's mission – a missional grammar (see Roxburgh 2008, 96).

The DRC framework document argues convincingly:

By staying true to our reformed identity (*ecclesia reformata, semper reformanda*), the reformed church has now been brought before the challenge of adapting to the constantly changing context".

And...

"This massive change in context demands that we re-examine the church's ecclesiology and missiology, finding new and creative ways of thinking and being as Christians (NG Kerk 2013c).

My conclusion is that the balance between gatekeepers and traders is in the crucible of massive contextual changes and is being stirred by powerful convictions on the nature and identity of the DRC. The existing power relations, formed by the intrinsic relationship between language (especially formalized and institutionalized language) and power, and guarded by the custodians of formalized church language (*actuarii*), is under pressure and does not facilitate the expansive and transforming nature of a missional ecclesiology. The DRC must make identity-defining choices that do not allow the current understanding of the church order to control the church and keep it in the mode of 'business as usual'.

1.3. The priority of the reformed confessions of faith in the understanding of the drc's identity, and the relationship between the confessional and missional identity of the drc

The DRC has a self-understanding as a confessing church, and the way in which this finds expression in the church order indicates the defining role of confessions of faith in the DRC. The very first article states:

The Dutch Reformed Church is based on the Bible as the holy and infallible Word of God. The doctrine which the Church confesses, in agreement with the Word of God, is expressed in the Forms of Unity as formulated at the Synod of Dordt in 1618–19, namely the thirty-seven articles of the Belgic Confession, the Heidelberg Catechism and the five Canons of Dordt (NG Kerk 2013b, 1).

Strauss argues that these confessions represent the deepest articulation of the faith identity of the church, and that confessions therefore demand a very large majority, or broader agreement, to be accepted or changed (see Strauss 2013, 21). When a proposal served before the 2013 General Synod to formulate the core identity of the DRC in missional terms and to place this before the article that describes the confessional unity, the Synod rejected the proposal and stated that the confessional identity precedes the missional identity of the DRC.

This approach might create tension, as the DRC policy document (Framework Document) on the missional nature of the church clearly states:

- Firstly, the church is the direct result of God's mission, and from this beginning becomes a participant in God's mission.
- The church is mission and participates in God's mission. It simply cannot be anything other than that!
- The church is the result, the fruition, of God's mission, and therefore exists to take part in this mission and be of service to ensure its continuation (NG Kerk 2013c).

The nearly complete silence of the DRC confessions of faith on the missional nature of the church, and the current priority of these issues, clearly illustrates this tension (see also Granberg-Michaelson 2008, 277).

The DRC tried to ease this tension by adding a new article into the Church Order in 2013:

> The Dutch Reformed Church was established by the Triune God to participate in God's mission in the world. The church is equipped by the Holy Spirit to serve God's glory and to proclaim the ministry of reconciliation and salvation in Christ (NG Kerk 2013b, 1).

Although the article on the confessional identity precedes this article on the missional identity of the DRC, the numerical ordering of the articles does not necessarily imply a theological order. The real issue here is more about identity and the fact that a new missional era questions the very structures and roles created by the confessions of faith, and the context presupposed by the confessions of faith. Roxburgh argues that the way the core elements of denominational identity were put together to "... form the overall sense of ourselves is now failing" (Roxburgh 2008, 77). We must find ways to remember the founding narratives and grammar (confessions of faith), but also ways to legitimize the new missional grammar and imagination. This is indeed a new paradigm that recognizes the disruptions as the work of the triune God who, through the Spirit, is inviting the church into a new direction by moving it outside the gate, albeit it with a strong memory of its founding narrative (see Roxburgh 2008, 96). Keifert explains that it is not primarily an issue of faithfulness to the tradition: "To be faithful, you must also be faithful to the constituting moment of the church that comes, not from the past, but... from God's absolute future. Faithfulness is as much about faithfulness to God's future as it is faithfulness to God's past... " (Keifert 2006, 65–66)

My conclusion is that the missional transformation of the DRC poses a confessional challenge. The exact nature of the relationship between the confessional and missional identity of the DRC will only be discerned over time. Granberg-Michaelson, from the perspective of the Reformed Church in America, also underscores the importance of patience: "... it is essential to take time" (Granberg-

Michaelson 2008, 281). Malan Nel also argues for a long-term perspective in the missional transformation of the church (see Nel 2015, 81). It might necessitate a new confession of faith, as the current collection of confessions of faith does not help the DRC to learn what it means to be missional. A new and clear definition of a legitimating framework, that recognizes both the founding narratives as well as God's preferred future, will not crystallize in the foreseeable future. The adoption of such a framework document would imply that the DRC has entered a liminal space in terms of the transformation of the church's identity, a time that calls for bold humility.

2. How is the mission of the church served and/or hindered by church order?

Missional theology is built on the conviction that God has a mission, and his mission has a church. Mission precedes the church and calls the church into being to serve God's purposes in the world (Niemandt 2015a, 2). This must be expressed in church polity. Roxburgh correctly identified this as a question of legitimacy (see Roxburgh 2008, 80). Church polity, the power of written conventions and the resultant structural issues, can hinder the mission of the church. This can be seen in the following issues in the DRC.

2.1. The Christendom paradigm versus the missional paradigm, and the continued influence of the Christendom paradigm

The DRC found itself in a Christendom paradigm up until the political transformation in South Africa in 1994, and even for a considerable time after 1994. 'Christendom' refers to the metanarrative that defined church and state where society was assumed to be Christian. Christianity became a religious institution with its attendant structures, offices, and rituals (see Frost and Hirsch, 2003, 8). It is a situation where the Christian parish was a political and geographical area within which each person was considered a member. In many instances, the distinction between church and state disappeared, and cultural forces in society and the church became intertwined (see Keifert 2006, 31).

This also influenced the role of the minister/pastor. Keifert states that the Christendom paradigm had significant implications for congregations and the understanding of the role of pastors. Pastors became responsible for the maintenance of the congregation. They had to baptize, marry, and bury believers. In this paradigm, the church lost its apostolic and missionary character and focused on the maintenance of the system (*societas*).

This paradigm also characterized South African culture, and the DRC in the 20th century can be described as a typical Christendom church. This can be seen in the following articles of the church order:

- The way the DRC church order still enshrines the idea of a Christendom parish and the idea that each congregation has borders, and that DRC congregations collectively cover most of South Africa – where you find a postal code, you will find a DRC congregation (Reglement 21, point 2.1.4, 2.1.7 [NG Kerk 2013b, 91]; Reglement 23, point 1.1.3.2.1 [NG Kerk 2013b, 105], 1.1.6 [NG Kerk 2013b, 106]).
- The implicit assumption that the work of ministers is limited to this particular parish (the members of a particular congregation) in Article 10 (NG Kerk 2013b, 4). There was no need to see the pastor/minister as someone who had to be missionary – because the whole country was understood as being predominantly Christian.
- The assumption that any other work diminishes the calling or suitability of a pastor, and the limitations on pastors to do any other work in Article 11 (NG Kerk 2013b, 4).

The political changes in 1994, as well as the growing influence of postmodernism, changed much of this, but the remnants of this Christendom paradigm are still visible in the DRC. The DRC needs the same approach expressed in a new policy document of the *Protestantse Kerk in Nederland* (see PCN 2015), namely that 'open spaces' do exist and that these open spaces create missional opportunities. The Christendom paradigm, that implies the primary task of the pastor to be the maintenance of the congregation, needs to change into a more apostolic understanding of the office of the minister.

My conclusion is that there is a clear indication that the Christendom paradigm in the DRC is transforming into a missional paradigm, and that the uncomfortable identification between dominant culture and the DRC is disappearing. Some of this is visible in the departure from the strong focus on the parish as expression of church. See Reglement 21, point 2.1.4, which does not allow a congregation to serve outside the borders of the parish (NG Kerk 2013, 91). There is also a transformation in the understanding of the offices, and a reframing of the task of the minister/pastor (See Cordier and Niemandt 2014; also, Cordier and Niemandt, 2015). One must, however, be aware of the strong and lingering influence of the Christendom paradigm, and take cognizance of the remnants of this era in the current church order, as well as many of the church structures of the DRC.

2.2. *The way in which the church order vests power in the pastor and parish (with specific reference to the immobility of pastors and the problems created for potential new church plants)*

The power structures in the DRC have been characterized by a strong focus on the local congregation as complete expression of church (*ecclesia completans)*, and the relativc autonomy of local pastors and congregational governance (Consistory = *Kerkraad*). Up until recently, pastors chaired the consistory, and – with the exception of regular visitation – the powerful combination of minister and consistory had considerable autonomy. Broader structures cannot do much to determine or direct ministry or mission in the parish.

A second issue is the lack of any apostolic focus in the description of the work of a pastor, and a heavy emphasis on pastoral, teaching, and leadership aspects of ministry. The passionate plea of Hirsch comes to mind, where he argues that all functions of the church must be qualified by its mission to extend the redemptive mission of God through its life and witness: "The apostolic leader thus embodies, symbolizes, and *re*-presents the apostolic mission to the missional community" (Hirsch 2006, 152). It is interesting to note the important changes in the PCN (see PCN 2015, 28), and the call in the *Vision 2025* document to allow a more apostolic understanding of the office of pastor:

The minister anno 2025 is called into a post-Christian culture, in a missionary situation. More than ever, the minister will need to be informed by the image of the apostle, in addition to that of the pastor, to proclaim the gospel in this world.

The PCN addresses the issue of the immobility of ministers in their discussion of a more apostolic understanding of the office, and argues that the richness and depth of the Gospel demands a regular change in pastors (see PCN 2015, 28).

The DRC does have a similar situation, with a high percentage of ministers being in the same congregation for longer than 10 years. The issue of mobility demands special attention, and the 2015 General Synod tried to put measures in place that will enhance mobility, and facilitate easier circulation of pastors (NG Kerk 2015a, 358). Early, but not yet sufficient, signs of a shift towards a more apostolic formulation of the office of minister is also evident in the current church order. It states that the pastor is responsible for leadership in worship, building up the congregation, education and equipping the faithful, the service ministry of the congregation, leadership in and organization of the congregation, love and discipline, pastoral care and the development of appropriate skills in the congregation. Church planting has been added by the 2013 synod (NG Kerk 2013b, 4). The emphasis of this description is still very much on the teaching and pastoral dimensions of ministry, and not the missional dimension.

A third issue is the fact that new church plants in the DRC are nearly non-existent. Although I am personally aware of more than 10 new church plants by DRC ministers, all of these ministers had to leave the DRC, with their new churches in tow, because of issues regarding church polity and difficulties in embracing new – especially different than usual (I refer here to the type of church plants generally described as 'Fresh Expressions' of church – churches that incarnate into the dominant culture of the day, but that do not conform to that culture (see Nell and Grobler 2014, 747–768)) – types of church plants. Recent changes in the DRC polity only begin to address this issue, but the DRC is far from being a dual-economy church that encourages, enables, and facilities new church plants.

My conclusion is that the current church polity still enshrines much of the power in the minister and a particular understanding of the church parish, framed by a Christendom paradigm, and that many potential church plants and missional initiatives are stymied because of this. There is no real mixed-economy understanding of the church ('Mixed-economy' refers to the co-existence of parish churches with new expressions of church that do not have the constraints of parish borders and Christendom (see Fresh Expressions 2016)), although the DRC has officially partnered with the Fresh Expressions initiative (see Fresh Expressions South Africa 2016).

2.3. A church order and polity that reflects ecclesiology and guides the drc to imagine a future beyond itself to participate in the activity of the Triune God in this world

The church order must reflect the particular ecclesiology of the DRC. What the church *is* determines what the church *does*. The purpose of the church and the direction and scope of its ministries are determined by the nature and character of the church (Niemandt 2015a, 2). Church polity, both in terms of the formal expression in the church order, as well as the application in the denominational system, must guide the DRC to imagine a missional future, and allow that imagination to form church praxis. It must legitimize a missional ecclesiology. I have referred to the power of words and narratives, and the fact that the church order determines power and power relations in the DRC. Texts, especially institutionalized texts or discourses such as church orders, constitute church practice. It forms part of the narrative that provides an explanatory framework that addresses the church's identity and understanding of church life.

Missional ecclesiology compels the church to live in God's preferred and promised future (see Keifert 2006, 64). The DRC is aware of this significant shift, and therefore states in their framework document: "Our reformed identity places the DRC within the 'life of the Triune God'. Any reflection on the identity of the church thus has to begin with consideration as to what it means to live in a relationship with God" (NG Kerk 2013c).

Keifert also argues that the nature of the church must be shaped by the living, triune God. The brings the question of God's preferred and promised future into the equation. Nel says that the challenge is to not be caught in the black hole of preservation and restoration, but rather the continued reformation in line with the will of God (see Nel 2015, 88). Keifert sees this very issue as the solution to the tension between gatekeepers (with the focus on the past and faithfulness to the tradition) and traders (with the focus on the new and visionary). Keifert argues that to be faithful the church must be faithful to the constituting moment of the church that comes, not from the past, but from God's absolute future. Our God is a living, triune God who dwells in all times, and in the life of God all times are present – the church participates in the already but not yet of that once and future life of God. He pleads: "Thus the question of faithfulness is not past vs. future but finding a useable past for our faithfulness to God's preferred and promised future" (Keifert 2006, 66).

The missional identity of the church changes everything. Janse van Rensburg argues that the adoption of the framework document and the priority of a missional understanding of church changes the life of the church on four levels: 1) the personal lives of church members, 2) on the level of congregational life, 3) denominational identity and, 4) the role of the church in society. It will eventually change faith practices, worship and liturgy, church planting policies and practices, church polity, and the focus of the church on human dignity in broader society (see Janse van Rensburg 2016).

My conclusion is that the development of a theological and ecclesiological framework on the missional identity of the church (perhaps in the form of a new confession of faith), as well as the re-imagining of church polity and the eventual design of an appropriate and legitimizing church polity, is of the utmost importance. This missional polity seeks to legitimize and organize church life in the best way possible to reflect its theological foundations and missional future.

2.4. A permission-giving church polity that allows a missional imagination to flourish, and focuses on getting out of the way of the missional momentum of congregations

If missional church means "finding out where the Holy Spirit is at work and joining in" (Kim 2009, 1), the structure and organization of the church, and church polity, must be open-ended. Granberg-Michaelson describes this as a "procedural challenge" (Granberg-Michaelson 2008, 280) and argues that the Reformed tradition built much of its governing structures around the principle of mistrust. I have argued elsewhere that good governance entails a church polity that is conducive towards the transformation of the church into missional life (see Niemandt 2015a, 2). Finding a useable past for our faithfulness to God's preferred and promised future implies an openness to the future, and to the work of God. The work of the Holy Spirit can never be pre-empted. Brewin uses complexity theory in his description of the Christian faith and the church (see Brewin 2013, loc.1096–1280). His description of characteristics of emergent systems fits the complexity of denominational and congregational church systems very well:

- They are open to their environment: sensing it, responding to it. They have blurred boundaries rather than fixed lines, and are characterized by disequilibrium rather than homeostasis.
- They adapt themselves to its unique and localized needs. They will be open places, fully engaging with the environment that is hosting it, sensing it, responding to it, learning from it, always seeking to change and evolve.
- They are learning systems in a cycle of sensing, learning, adapting, and changing.
- They have distributed knowledge that is dispersed over a large variety of agents.

Keifert also argues for open systems that focus on a joining and belonging sociology: "They have permeable boundaries rather than the high boundaries of closed systems" (Keifert 2006, 144).

Bandy passionately argues that thriving churches no longer assume that God blesses structure and control above all else in church organization (see Bandy 1999, 26). He juxtaposes a hierarchical controlling organization with a team-based, streamlined and permissive organization (see Bandy 1999, 32). Bandy proposes a permission-giving church, an organizational approach that thinks proscriptively (and thus open-ended) (see Bandy 1999, 63f.). He argues that proscriptive allows for speed, creativity, and relevance. The structure and polity of these kinds of churches focus on core values, beliefs, vision, and mission, and on the reshaping of general policy (see Bandy 1999, 35). Prescriptive thinking drives the organization to err on the side of control. Proscriptive thinking drives the organization to err on the side of freedom. But, says Bandy: "... it is the clarity and balance between prescriptive and proscriptive thinking that lies at the heart of the thriving church organization" (Bandy1999, 36).

My conviction is that such a permission-giving church polity will allow the missional imagination to flourish and will facilitate a church order that gets out of the way of the missional momentum of congregations. It acknowledges the New Testament lessons about giftedness and embracing the gift of leadership and discernment. Proscriptive polity is the only way to facilitate experimenting with change that engages deep cultural transformation in denominational life (see Keifert 2006, 81).

A permission-giving church order will:

- Recognize the mystery that God is in charge and that it is neither the members nor the leaders of the church who are in charge (cf. Janse van Rensburg, who argues: "The DRC needs to open up new spaces of deeper discernment and a commitment to be aware of the presence of God"; and "There will be no missional movement without a first-hand witness on the presence of the living God" (see Janse van Rensburg 2016));
- Allow change and facilitate moves out of the modus of 'business as usual';
- Nurture a climate of discernment;
- Show a willingness to share a journey, although the final destination might not be crystal-clear;
- Embrace ambiguity.

2.5. A church order that facilitates faithful presence in the parish

I have been critical of the parish system as a remnant of Christianity. My conviction is that the DRC needs a church order that recognizes the importance of the 'new commons', or 'new parish', and that the church order must facilitate 'faithful presence in the parish'. 'New commons' refers to the space that serves the interests of the community, and where the resources are used for the sake of the common good. Sparks *et al.* argues that humans are meant to share life together, to learn to fit together as a living body in relationship with God, with one another, and for the place to which they are called (see Sparks *et al.* 2014, 18). When we use what we own, the idea of the commons demands that we are obliged to think about our neighbors, because we share life with these others (Niemandt 2015b, 336–348). The commons is the space where life is shared with the lives of others – "the theatre in which the life of the community is played out" (Brewin 2012, loc. 715). This is very much what others call the "new parish" (Sparks *et al.* 2014). It refers to all the relationships (including the land) where the local church lives out its faith together (Sparks *et al.* 2014, 23).

Sparks *et al.* argue that Christendom practice was the move away from localized presence to centralized power within a hierarchical church system: "This shift away from being rooted in a particular parish had the unintended consequence of church authorities living above their place and dictating how people at the local level should behave. The technique of enforcing religious tradition and the standardization of belief forever altered the state of the church" (Sparks *et al.* 2014, 40).

A 'new parish' differs from a 'Christendom parish' in the sense that it is not determined by geographical borders, but by a process of communal discernment as the common space and place where a particular congregation can be faithfully present (Sparks *et al.* 2014, 68).

Sparks *et al.* describe faithful presence as follows: "'Faithful presence' is a phrase that describes this relational view of the world. It means that in each situation we are listening for what our relationships require of us and responding according to our capacity. Each relationship might require a nuanced response" (Sparks *et al.* 2014, 59)

Faithful presence is to be able discern the mission of God in everyday life, to join in with the Spirit, and to serve each other and the community so that life can flourish. It includes the challenge to turn the agenda away from purely private gain to public benefit (see Niemandt 2015b, 342). Sparks *et al.* explain it in terms of the following:

- Community focuses on developing a common life together in the way of Christ. This includes knowing and being known by God and one another. It also means recognizing that each person has unique gifts to bring to the life of the body.
- Formation has to do with developing the practices and postures that shape us into mature people of faith both personally and collectively.
- Mission is bearing witness to the love of Jesus and the reign of God. It is joining the Spirit's movement in the neighborhood and seeking the reconciliation and renewal of all things (see Sparks et al. 2014, 85–86).

My conclusion is that a new church order for the DRC must be a permission-giving order that allows faithful presence in the new parish. The PCN pleaded for a church order that recognizes 'open spaces' (see PCN 2015), as well as a new kind of presence in familiar spaces. The territorial principle cannot be maintained, and the church order must facilitate a system that allows a unity in diversity, not based on territorial boundaries, but embracing diversity in terms of cultures, spiritualties, and demographic profiles.

3. Conclusion

The DRC has embarked on a journey of missional transformation. At this stage, there is sufficient clarity and consensus on the nature of the church as a missional community participating in God's mission to compel the denomination to make significant changes to its church order. These changes need to deconstruct the power relations implicit in the current church order, and must facilitate a new missional dispensation and praxis. The point of orientation thus shifts from the primacy of the church's past to God's preferred future, from a prescriptive to a proscriptive church order, and from territorial boundaries to faithful presence in open spaces. The new missional church order can serve God's mission and the DRC, legitimize change, and assist the denomination to adopt a posture of service in bold humility rather than power and preservation.

Abbreviations and bibliography

CO-DRC:
Church Order of the Dutch Reformed Church
CO-DRCA:
Church Order of the Dutch Reformed Church in Africa
CO-URCSA:
Church Order of the Uniting Reformed Church in Southern Africa
DRC: Dutch Reformed Church
DRCA: Dutch Reformed Church in Africa
DRMC: Dutch Reformed Mission Church
RCA: Reformed Church in Africa
URCSA: Uniting Reformed Church in Southern Africa

Bandy, Thomas G. 1999. Christian chaos: Revolutionizing the congregation. Nashville: Abingdon.

Brewin, Kester. 2012. Mutiny! Why we love pirates, and how they can save us. Vaux: Kindle edition.

Brewin, Kester. 2013. The complex Christ: Signs of emergence in the urban church. Vaux: Kindle edition.

Cordier, Gert, and Cornelius J.P. Niemandt. 2014. The minister as missional leader (1). In: Journal for Missional Practice, 5(2014).

Cordier, Gert, and Cornelius J.P. Niemandt. 2015. The minister as missional leader (2). In: Journal for Missional Practice, 6(2015).

Dingemans, Gijs D.J. 1987. Een huis om in te wonen: Schetsen en bouwstenen voor een Kerk en een Kerkorde van de toekomst. 's-Gravenhage: Uitgeverij Boekencentrum.

Frost, Michael, and Alan Hirsch. 2003. The shaping of things to come: Innovation and mission for the 21st-century church. Peabody: Hendrickson.

Fairclough, Norman. 1992. Discourse and social change, 2nd Ed. Cambridge: Polity Press.

Fairclough, Norman. 2013. Language and power, 2nd Ed. Abingdon: Routledge.

Fresh Expressions. 2016. Accessed March 15, 2016. https://www.freshexpressions.org.uk/guide/about/mixedeconomy

Fresh Expressions South Africa. 2016. Accessed March 15, 2016. http://freshexpressions.co.za

Granberg-Michaelson. 2008. Insights into becoming a missional denomination: The Reformed Church in America. In: Van Gelder, Craig (ed.). 2008. The missional church & denominations: Helping congregations develop a missional identity. Pages 265–282. Grand Rapids: Eerdmans.

Hirsch, Alan. 2006. The forgotten ways: Reactivating the missional church. Grand Rapids: Brazos Press.

Jackson, Neels. 2016. 21 Appèlle teen besluite oor gays. Accessed March 15, 2016. http://kerkbode.christians.co.za/2016/03/15/21-appelle-teen-besluite-oor-gays/.

Janse van Rensburg, Nelis. 2016. Gestuurdheid vra 'n paradigmaskuif. Accessed February 19, 2016. http://kerkbode.christians.co.za/2016/02/19/gestuurdheid-vra-n-paradigmaskuif/.

Keifert, Patrick. 2006. We are here now: A new missional era. Eagle: Allelon.

Kim, Kirsteen. 2009. Joining in with the Spirit: Connecting world church and local mission. London: Epworth.

Koffeman, Leo J. 2009. Het goed recht van de kerk: Een theologische inleiding op het kerkrecht. Kampen: Kok.

Nederduitse Gereformeerde Kerk [NGK]. 2013a. Agenda vir die 15de vergadering van die Algemene Sinode van die Nederduitse Gereformeerde Kerk 2013, 06–10 Oktober 2013. Pretoria: NG Kerk.

Nederduitse Gereformeerde Kerk [NGK]. 2013b. Die Kerkorde van die Nederduitse Gereformeerde Kerk met Reglemente, Beleid, Funksionele Besluite en Riglyne soos vasgestel deur die Algemene Sinode in Oktober 2013. Pretoria: NG Kerk.

Nederduitse Gereformeerde Kerk [NGK]. 2013c. Framework document on the missional nature and calling of the DRC. Pretoria: NG Kerk. http://www.ngkerkas.co.za/wp-content/uploads/2013/04/FRAMEWORK-DOCUMENT-ON-THE-MISSIONAL-NATURE-AND-CALLING-OF-THE-DUTCH-REFORMED-CHURCH.doc.

Nederduitse Gereformeerde Kerk [NGK]. 2015(a). Agenda vir die 16de vergadering van die Algemene Sinode van die Nederduitse Gereformeerde Kerk 2015, 04–09 Oktober 2015. Pretoria: NG Kerk.

Nederduitse Gereformeerde Kerk [NGK]. 2015(b). Notule van die Eerste vergadering van die Algemene Sinode Moderamen, 16–18 November 2015. Pretoria: NG Kerk.

Nederduitse Gereformeerde Kerk [NGK]. 2015(c). Besluiteregister 16de vergadering van die Algemene Sinode van die Nederduitse Gereformeerde Kerk 2015, 04–09 Oktober 2015. Pretoria: NG Kerk.

Nel, Malan. 2015. Identity-driven churches. Who we are, and where are we going? Wellington: Biblecor.

Nell, Ian, and Rudolph Grobler. 2014. An exploration of fresh expressions as missional church: Some practical-theological perspectives. In: NGTT 55(2014)/3 and 4: 747–768.

Niemandt, Cornelius J.P. 2014. Emerging Missional Ecclesiology in the Dutch Reformed Church in South Africa and Church Polity. In: Janssen, Allan J., and Leo J. Koffeman (eds.). 2014. Protestant Church Polity in Changing Contexts, 65–82. Zurich: LitVerlag.

Niemandt, Cornelius J.P. 2015a. Together towards life and mission: A basis for good governance in church and society today. In: Verbum et Ecclesia 36(2015)/1: 10 pages. Accessed March 10, 2016. http://dx.doi.org/10.4102/ve.v36i1.1361.

Niemandt, Cornelius J.P. 2015b. Together towards life: Sailing with pirates. In: Missionalia 43(2015)/3: 336–348.

Protestantse Kerk Nederland [PCN]. 2015. Kerk 2015: Waar een Woord is, is een weg. http://www.protestantsekerk.nl/overons/protestantse-kerk/kerk-2025/Paginas/intro.aspx.

Roxburgh, Alan. 2008. Reframing Denominations from a Missional Perspective. In Van Gelder, Craig (ed.). 2008. The missional church & denominations: Helping congregations develop a missional identity. Pages 75–103. Grand Rapids: Eerdmans.

Strauss, Piet. 2013. Kerkwees in die branding: Die Nederduitse Gereformeerde Kerk in Algemene Sinodale verband 1994 – 2011. Bloemfontein: Acta Theologica Supplementum 18.

Sparks, Paul, Tim Soerens, and Dwight J. Friesen. 2014. The New Parish: How Neighborhood Churches Are Transforming Mission, Discipleship and Community. Downers Grove: InterVarsity Press.

CHURCH POLITY AS AN AGENT OF UNITY IN THE CHURCH

Kathy Smith

A CASE STUDY FROM THE CHRISTIAN REFORMED CHURCH IN NORTH AMERICA

Introduction

What are the mission and the polity of the church? How do the church's mission and polity relate to each other? Does polity bring unity to the church, so that it can go forward in its mission? Or does polity bring disunity as churches argue over issues, rules and procedures, hindering the church from accomplishing its mission?

In my denomination, the Christian Reformed Church in North America (CRC), both of these voices can be heard, as I'm sure is true in many denominations. I recently spoke at a CRC classis meeting, and both views were represented in the delegates present. Some were sticklers for doing things 'by the book', and others scoffed at the idea that polity could be anything but a straitjacket when it comes to ministry.

Many people view polity as a dam that obstructs ministry. Others want to use polity to keep the water in the reservoir, all decently and in good order. But neither extreme is helpful. If we view polity as an agent of unity in the church, we will find that it can make room for mission and ministry to flow. Polity can also be the means by which we sort out instances of disunity so that the flow of ministry is *not* hindered. So polity actually can facilitate the mission of the church.

To explore the relationship of church polity to the unity of the church, we will consider four related questions. First, we will ask whether polity is necessary, and why we need it in the church. Second, we will consider how polity can be an agent of unity in this world and how it helps the church fulfill its mission. Third, we will look at how polity can disentangle instances of disunity in the church and help to bring consensus and restore unity. And finally, we will reflect on how a dynamic understanding of polity can make room for mission and ministry to flow.

Is Polity Necessary?

We begin with the first of four questions: Is polity necessary? Do we need it? Recently I was teaching church polity to a group of college students who aspired to be worship leaders, explaining the importance of understanding the poli*tics* and the poli*ty* of their churches, especially in difficult situations. One student wondered if polity has a positive side and asked a pointed question: "Will there be polity in heaven?" I paused a moment and responded, "Yes, I think so. Even though we shouldn't have to deal with the kinds of disagreements we face in this life, there still will be people with different roles and a need for some way to bring unity and organization to our worship and service".

Now, since there won't be sin in heaven, it may be hard to imagine that organization or order will be needed. Theologically, is order needed due to sin, or is it needed for unity in the body of Christ and effectiveness in that body's functioning?

Even when people are getting along fine, they can benefit from being organized well. Leadership and laws in this world exist not only to keep order by stopping crime or dysfunction, but also to help people live well and work well together. So I can imagine having polity in heaven, if we understand it as a way of organizing people for doing good.

What will be absent in heaven is *resistance* to order. Many of the problems I see in the churches I consult with are not due to problems with the church order itself, but are related to whether the church order is being interpreted or implemented well. It's usually the behavior of people or churches that is problematic. And frankly, most of the problems are due to sinful human nature and an inability to get along well—factors which will not be problems in heaven.

But let's get back down to earth.

How can polity be an agent of unity in this world?

The purpose of church polity is to provide wise ways of living together as the body of Christ in this world. The documents of church polity – books of order or canon law – may seem like legal documents, but they really fall into the genre of wisdom literature. Polity does involve rules and regulations, but those provisions (a preferable word) are in place because they represent the wisdom of the church – wisdom about how things work well, and how we can order ourselves in ways that reflect God's will in the Scriptures.

Polity helps the church to fulfill its mission – to function as a group of worshiping communities that are engaged in faith formation and fellowship with the missional goal of spreading the gospel. Polity provides structures to support that purpose, but also allows for the flexibility and diversity within those structures that will help to preserve the unity of the church. Church polity offers a framework for worship, faith nurture, and pastoral care, all so that the mission of the church can go forward. Even provisions for membership and discipline are meant to encourage the flourishing of the body of Christ – so that the gospel will go out. And the many provisions related to ordination and office also serve the ultimate purpose that Christ's rule be carried out to the churches and into the world. Those provisions need to include flexibility because the church needs to discern its context well, and have the freedom to adjust to that context.

For example, initiatives to plant new congregations are given room to grow by the CRC's Church Order. It allows the flexibility needed for mission to flow by not requiring emerging churches to follow all the provisions of polity, recognizing that church planters need to be creative and entrepreneurial in starting a church. This creativity ought to have a purpose in mind, though, and that goal should be to eventually organize as a congregation of the denomination supporting it. So, wisdom would call for these new churches to gradually develop traits and practices similar to those in the Church Order, so they don't come as a surprise when it is time to officially organize as regular congregations, after which they are obligated to follow the provisions of the Church Order.

I teach my students that Reformed polity should be built into the plan for a church plant from the beginning. Leaders should be accountable to a leadership team or steering committee and should begin to develop roles similar to those of elder and deacon. Church planters should teach and preach within the bounds of the doctrines that the CRC affirms, and develop a commitment to those doctrines among leaders especially, but also all members. They will be less likely to face resistance when the time comes to officially organize if the transition to full standing as a congregation will not change them in ways counter to their development. Following polity should not deter church plants from organizing, but simply put words on structures they are already developing. This then is one way that polity brings unity – by allowing flexibility for new churches to develop an identity that is recognizably Christian Reformed as they grow in new contexts.

Another way that polity brings unity is by grounding the church in the Christian creeds and the Reformed confessions. Holding to the Apostle's, Nicene, and Athanasian Creeds ties us to the attributes of the one, holy, catholic, and apostolic church. Church polity calls us to unity as we abide by our mutually agreed upon rules, but also as we work together to change those rules, if needed. Polity calls us to holiness as we observe its principles and submit to the authority of the church and its provisions for corrective discipling when we stray from them. Polity calls us to be a catholic and apostolic church in its provisions for recognizing the variety of congregations and our place within the wider Christian church, and in its provisions for extending the mission and ministries of the church.

Further, holding to the Reformed confessions leads to specific provisions that flow from our theologies of ordination, liturgy, education, and mission. For example, the Reformed confessions include the doctrine of infant baptism, and Christian Reformed congregations practice infant baptism as a sign and seal of what God has done in the lives of children of believers. In fact, we see it as a beautiful image of God's role in salvation and our receiving that gift even though we could not choose it. This confessionally-grounded practice is required by our Church Order, and alternative practices have been discouraged by our synod—the only body that can change the Church Order.

Finally, Reformed polity's goal to be an agent of unity is made clear in specific language we use to describe how church order is designed to function in the Christian Reformed Church. In the Reformed tradition, we talk about 'covenanting together'. The introduction to the Church Order of the Christian Reformed Church says it is "more than a contractual set of regulations or simply guidelines ... , it really is a record of our covenanting together within this denominational fellowship". The introduction goes on: "As leaders and members and congregations of the CRCNA, we promise to use these regulations to order our life together as a particular part of the body of Christ. And that covenant commitment is based on our belief that Christ is the head of the church and we, as Christ's body, must reflect Christ in how we function, choose leaders, assemble, deliberate over issues, carry out the ministries and mission of the church, and hold one another accountable for all these things. We agree to abide by these promises and to work together to change the regulations when necessary. It's important to remember that the Church Order is a document of the churches, and what it says and how it changes is determined by the churches together. It's our book; in a sense, we all are its authors. And as our denomination becomes more diverse, the Church Order helps to build unity by establishing normative patterns even as it encompasses many different churches in varying local contexts" (CO-CRCNA, 7).

One of the characteristics of the Christian Reformed Church is a fierce loyalty to the denomination and a strong commitment to not 'disobey' the denomination. This 'covenanting together' is more than words in our Church Order, and is all the more reason that the denomination needs to be careful not to overstep its regulative function, and not bind the conscience and behavior of the church except in areas that truly go to the heart of the denomination's identity.

One specific feature of this 'covenanting together' is mutual accountability, which becomes a mechanism for unity. Church members and office-bearers are accountable to each other and to one another in our polity. Likewise, congregations are accountable to each other and to their classes and to the synod. In our system of broader assemblies, the local churches and regional classes send delegates and also delegate authority to those bodies to make decisions which are then binding to the churches. So it is crucial for the deliberations in the broader assemblies to include the whole spectrum of viewpoints in the church, and to debate them while all are listening to the leading of Christ's Spirit, as Christ rules the church.

How does polity disentangle instances of disunity?

It is unavoidable that disagreements will arise regarding how best to carry out the mission and how to shape the ministries of the church, much less how to manage practical issues of church membership, ministerial credentials, elections to office, access to and administration of the sacraments, and a whole host of other specific matters. Without some type of order, such differences would threaten to undo us, but in a system of covenanting together, polity becomes an agent of unity that keeps us together in times of disunity. Rather than simply going our own way, we agree to follow our polity in having these discussions in orderly ways. Further, if the point of disagreement is actually our polity itself, we have procedures by which to propose and approve of changes to the process and to the Church Order.

Another way polity brings order and unity to churches is in dealing with controversial issues, though it could be that the methodology needs to change in terms of exactly how those discussions happen. Some denominations are finding that the most difficult issues require more time and conversation, not just appointing a study committee to produce a report that has recommendations which can be debated and voted up or down. In the CRC, we are beginning to value using a 'shepherding committee' that shepherds the conversation regarding an issue over a number of years, making proposals and changes along the way, allowing a gradual approach, and some possibilities for local options when it comes to implementation. It's a methodology that values differences and helps a church to hold together in spite of those differences.

Shepherding committees have worked best when the outcome includes different ways to implement a particular issue, while holding together on a consensus of deeper principles. For instance, in the Christian Reformed Church, we honor the fact that the Spirit gives gifts to all believers, but also honor differences between churches that believe both men and women should serve in leadership roles in the church and those that believe such roles are limited to men. In 1957, congregations were allowed to choose when to have women voting in congregational meetings – the denominational decision was to allow it, but to let congregations implement it on their own schedule. For some, that took decades, but they did it at their own pace.

In dealing with the issue of women in ecclesiastical office, the CRC first came to a compromise in 1995 that allowed classes to take exception to the 'male rule' and, honoring their own convictions, allow churches to ordain women. When more than half of the classes took exception to the rule, the denomination changed it, but still honors differences, now in the other direction. The 'male rule' was removed from the Church Order in 2007, but regional classes are now allowed to not have ordained women office-bearers as delegates to their meetings, according to their local convictions. At the general synod, they have to be willing to work alongside women delegated by other regions, but even there, they are allowed to register their protest. These changes in procedure were carefully processed through our polity, finding a way to keep the unity of the church.

Another example of allowing for differences is that in 2011 the CRC decided to allow admission of all baptized members to the Lord's Supper, including children and young people, without requiring a profession of faith first. But, understanding that a change like this may be very difficult for some churches, the CRC also allowed the churches to implement this decision under the supervision of their own elders. So, a lot of room was given for different practices, including the option of continuing to require a formal profession of faith before partaking of communion. And again, unity was preserved regarding a potentially divisive issue.

The big test will be whether the CRC can hold together in unity with a diversity of views on the issue of same-sex marriage, over which other denominations have split. The current position of the CRC is that same-sex orientation is not sinful, but same-sex behavior is, and so persons who are not heterosexually oriented are called to celibacy. That position was set in 1973 and still stands, although there are a variety of views about it in the denomination today, including some taking new looks at Scripture. The question is: can we once again find a way to allow for disagreement, and not sacrifice our unity?

On that issue, and whatever others may come our way, there should be room to find consensus at a deep enough level to hold us at the center. Hopefully we will be able to affirm that our unity in Christ is deeper than our position on polarizing issues and will realize a deeper commitment to stay together for the sake of ministry – the argument that finally brought a compromise on the women in office issue – and not split apart over these differences.

Finally, how can polity make room for mission and ministry to flow?

I conclude by noting a couple of things about a dynamic understanding of polity in the Christian Reformed Church that not only allows but expects synodical decisions and even the Church Order to change as churches and contexts change. In fact, our historical principles call us to have as few rules as possible and to change them as needed so they will be fitting and so that ministry and mission will continue to flow.

John Calvin encouraged this dynamic approach and gave wise advice for how to determine fitting changes. In his Institutes he wrote about rules and procedures that, "because these things are not necessary to salvation, and for the upbuilding of the church ought to be variously accommodated to the customs of each nation and age, it will be fitting … to change and abrogate traditional practices and to establish new ones. Indeed, I admit that we ought not to charge into innovation rashly, suddenly, for insufficient cause. But love will best judge what may hurt or edify; and if we let love be our guide, all will be safe" (Calvin 1559, 4.10.30).

That's the main point for our polity. As we do our best to follow Christ's leading and discern the missional calling of the church today, we need to do it as the one body of Christ. If we affirm our unity without sacrificing diversity, we will be able to see our way through any issue that comes our way. And if we let love be our guide, all will be safe.

Abbreviations and bibliography

CO-CRCNA:
Christian Reformed Church in North America. 2016. Church order and its supplements. Grand Rapids Mi: Christian Reformed Church in North America.
CRC: Christian Reformed Church in North America

Calvin, John. 1559. Institutes of the Christian Religion. Two volumes. Edited by John T. McNeill. Translation Ford Lewis Battles 1960. Philadelphia: The Westminster Press – London: SCM.

POLITY: PERILS AND PROMISES

Clyde Steckel

A CASE HISTORY: THE UNITED CHURCH OF CHRIST IN THE USA

Introduction and thesis

As the historic churches of European ancestry move onto the shifting terrain of global Christianity and confront their waning influence in post-modernity, the ways these churches are governed, or their polities, hold clues to renewal that may be overlooked. While aggressive marketing or doctrinal clarity may seem better ways to regain lost ground, reexamining church polity may in fact hold greater promise for both renewal and a revitalized ecumenism. My thesis in this paper is this: examining the trajectory of polity in the denomination called the United Church of Christ in the USA (UCC) yields important clues to polity's perils and promises. This will be a case history of one Protestant denomination's discoveries about uniting disparate polities and eventually creating something new in the annals of church governance.

Historical background

As a denomination born in 1957 at its Uniting General Synod, the UCC combined disparate polities as well as differing cultural and ecclesial traditions. The Congregational and Christian denomination was grounded in English Puritanism and Independence as well as American Puritan and Free Church movements. Its polity was fiercely congregational. Its uniting partner, the Evangelical and Reformed Church, came from German and Swiss Reformed as well as Lutheran traditions. Its polity was presbyterial. Observers within and outside these denominations wondered whether such a union could work and why it was being attempted.

These questions can be answered briefly, though the uniting process was lengthy and filled with risk, partly because of polity negotiations. The brief explanation goes like this: in the 1930s a small group of pastors and professors from the two denominations began meeting for biblical and theological study in St. Louis,

Missouri. With a worldwide Protestant ecumenical zeal prevailing then, and with a growing sense that these two denominations brought gifts mutually enriching, these St. Louis clergy proposed a union of these two denominations, a proposal that gradually gained the support of national denominational leaders.

Polity, however, was a sticking point. Anti-merger Congregationalists argued that the values of liberty and freedom of conscience inherent in congregational polity would be lost in such a union. Thus polity became more openly an article of faith than it was before. Congregationalists had taken their polity for granted, especially in its New England expression, where church polity and local governmental bodies were virtually synonymous. With the union negotiations, Congregationalists feared losing an essential element of its beliefs. One Congregational church even brought suit in federal court to terminate union negotiations, but eventually the appellate court allowed the union to proceed (see for this story: Gunnemann 1977, and Bendroth 2015).

The founding document called *The Basis of Union* was eventually approved by the synods of the Evangelical and Reformed Church and a sufficient number of local churches in the Congregational and Christian Churches to declare the union in effect at the uniting General Synod of 1957. The question of whether such a church union could survive has been answered affirmatively, with the UCC anticipating its 60th anniversary in 2017. But what kind of polity could there be for denominations united but with one previously governed presbyterially and the other governed congregationally? To answer that question we must examine what the first Constitution and Bylaws had to say about polity, and then how polity thinking and practices evolved across the years.

Polity in process: from congregational to covenantal

At the time of the Uniting General Synod of 1957 many details of the union remained to be completed, including writing and approving a Constitution. Many were nervous, especially Congregationalists, about declaring union without first approving a constitution. But the commitment to church union was strong enough then to agree to unite trusting that divine guidance would assist the process of working out the details. When the Constitution and Bylaws were declared in force in 1961, the polity set forth in those documents was clearly a congregational polity modified only by admonitions to listen to and take seriously the advice of regional and national denominational bodies. Paragraph 15 (now number 18 in the current Constitution) declared the inviolable autonomy of the local church, including the right to call its pastor, own its property, determine its covenants of faith and order its ways of worship. This inviolable autonomy was, however, qualified in principle by the Constitutional definitions of the powers of Associations (regional organizations of churches and ministers) to determine the standing of ministers and local churches in paragraphs 40 and 41. Apparently that word, standing, did not raise sufficient alarm among those guarding local church autonomy to call attention to a potential conflict or to try to change the wording.

As these polity principles were put into practice, four distinct entities became involved: Committees on Ministry (sometimes Church and Ministry Committees) of Associations; Manuals on Ministry; a national body, the Council for Church and Ministry; and Conference or Association Ministers.

Committees on Ministry: These were committees of Associations, whose task was guiding candidates for ordained, commissioned or licensed ministers; and reviewing the standing of ministers and churches.

Manuals on Ministry: Congregationalists were familiar with manuals offering counsel on common practices for guiding ministry committees and Conference/Association ministers. The current *Manual on Ministry* (1985) is a multivolume ring-binder. A new Manual is in the works at the time of this writing.

Council for Church and Ministry: This was a national agency providing resources for Association committees, including Manuals. Later this Council was dissolved and its duties transferred to a new Council for Church Life and Leadership. Now the comparable body is called Ministerial Excellence, Support and Authorization.

Conference or Association Ministers: Though these offices were not specified in the Constitution and Bylaws, the older offices of Conference Superintendent (Congregationalist) or Synod President (Evangelical and Reformed) were continued in the UCC as Conference or Association Ministers. They advise Committees on Ministry and worked with churches seeking a minister and ministers seeking a call.

Polity challenges across the decades

As UCC polity thinking and practices evolved in light of changing circumstances in church and society, the following issues took center stage, because they had not been foreseen by writers of the Constitution and Bylaws:

Transfers from other denominations: As American society increasingly divided over political issues like wars overseas and the reach of government, as well as social and moral issues such as racism, sexism, homophobia and abortion, some clergy and seminarians who held liberal or progressive views sought transfer to the UCC from denominations holding more conservative beliefs. Committees on Ministry had to distinguish between the risks and promises these transfers would bring.

Validating private, personal calls: Seekers and seminarians increasingly petitioned Committees on Ministry to validate their personal calls to ministry without assessing their gifts for ministry or whether the church had positions for the ministries they sought. Sometimes these seekers came from recovery experiences of drug or alcohol addiction or sexual abuse. Ministry committees and Association staff looked for ways to be both welcoming and to make it clear that ministry authorization was in and on behalf of the church, not just the person who feels called.

Creating disciplinary procedures for clergy and other church leaders: In the midst of growing public awareness of boundary violations and sexual abuse by clergy and other church leaders, Committees on Ministry needed guidelines and training in procedures fair to both accusers and the accused. A new section on disciplinary procedures was added to the *Manual on Ministry*. And Conference attorneys as well as a new national Office of General Counsel guided ministry committees in finding just and pastorally sensitive procedures for administering discipline.

Polity impeding ecumenism: From its beginning the UCC worked to foster a wider church union beyond its two uniting denominations. Would its polity and history of polity controversy become an impediment to achieving greater church unity? One aspect of its ecumenical calling, seeking mutual recognition of the sacraments and ministries of other denominations, was not troubled by polity differences. Among these were agreements of mutual recognition with churches having kinship ties with the UCC, such as those with the Evangelical Church of the Union in both East and West Germany in 1981. Polity was not an impediment since no changes in church governance were envisaged. Even with the 1997 *Formula of Agreement*, in which the Evangelical Lutheran Church in America, the Reformed Church in America, the Presbyterian Church in the USA and the UCC recognized the validity of the ministries and sacraments in all the churches of the Formula, their diverse polity practices were not impediments. Polity was similarly not an issue when the UCC pursued broader union with its near neighbor denomination, the Christian Church Disciples of Christ. In 1989 these two denominations entered into a mutual recognition of sacraments and ministries, framed as a Church Partnership.

But polity did become an impediment when the UCC received and then responded to historic documents seeking wider Christian unity. The first was the Lima Document of the World Council of Churches of 1982, titled *Baptism, Eucharist and Ministry* (BEM), in which member churches set forth areas of convergence on these historically church-dividing topics. Polity was also a divisive issue as the UCC responded to the Consensus of the Consultation on Church Union (COCU) of 1985. That was the foundational document for a projected ten-denomination organic union. Both these documents affirmed the ancient threefold ministries of bishops, presbyters and deacons. The UCC response to BEM was a cautiously worded agreement to consider the ancient threefold orders, while noting its own ways of conducting oversight and its puzzlement over the office of deacon. When it came time for the COCU uniting liturgy in 1999, Presbyterian and Episcopalian representatives disagreed about who should represent their churches in the opening ceremonial procession, with Episcopalians insisting on bishops or someone designated to that ministry but with Presbyterians insisting that their corporate oversight required committee processors, not a bishop surrogate. UCC representatives clearly supported the Presbyterian position, but held back, allowing Presbyterians to carry the argument. In the end COCU was dissolved, reconstituting itself in 2002 as Churches Uniting in Christ, with organic denominational union no longer the aim. Polity was not the only issue challenging COCU. The historically African American denominations insisted that racism in church and society should have greater priority than organic union. And across the years the ecumenical passion of earlier times had faded in the face of pressing moral and social justice issues.

Polity as a national denominational governance issue: When the UCC proposed to combine its multi-board national governance system into a single board structure in 2009, opponents cited UCC polity as an argument against doing that. Retaining a national governance structure with several independent boards helped disperse and share authority, these opponents argued, and provided more opportunities for under-represented minorities to be involved in key decisions. Because the Justice and Witness Ministry board vetoed the single board proposal, it was withdrawn from General Synod consideration. While the ethos of UCC polity favors broad participation, the polity itself should not have been cited as a reason to oppose single-board national governance, in my view.

A new ucc polity of covenant

Polity discourse in the UCC, in the years just discussed, increasingly spoke of covenantal polity, with fewer references to congregational polity. National executives and polity scholars began talking that way in the 1980s. This language had both descriptive and prescriptive force. Local churches no longer could claim absolute autonomy, with Association committees making binding decisions about candidates for ministry, disciplinary actions or regarding churches joining the UCC. Especially in the *Manual on Ministry* (1985) the language of covenant defines the relations between the candidate, the local church, the Committee on Ministry, and the ministry setting calling that person to an authorized ministry position. All these are partners in the covenant. By speaking of covenant, speakers and writers invoked the biblical concept of covenant, in which God calls and promises, respondents hear the call and promise to follow its terms, accountable finally to God and not just one another. While it may seem audacious or absurd philosophically or scientifically to claim that the God of the universe is intimately involved in such decisions, the Christian narrative, speaking of flowers of the field or birds of the air, promises, indeed requires such claims. At its best a covenantal polity depends on earnest prayer and bible study to make discerning decisions, though a vote may be required when discernment does not produce consensus.

Perils inherent in a polity of covenant are its uses that are moralistic or punitive, and the unanswered question of what to do when covenant partners fail to reach consensus even after the most devout prayer or protracted and respectful discussion. Moralism takes the form of accusations that one or more covenant partners failed to honor the covenant, though sometimes that simply means others failed to agree with accusers. Punitive decisions sometimes reflect the desire of covenant partners not to appear weak in the face of egregious behavior by a church or by a minister; or punitive decisions may simply reflect the collective attitude of covenant partners who want to punish but not rehabilitate.

The peril of dispersed authority also lurks in efforts to practice a covenantal polity. Who finally decides? How are decisions enforced? Implied in the ecclesiology of the UCC and other congregational polities is that decisions belong to the whole body of the church, not to an office of bishop or a representative assembly like a synod or presbytery. The practical limitations of such a polity are in clear view. Typically a difficult decision may be avoided altogether, or put off, or assigned to a new group. Covenantal polity needs to create and operate within a culture of mutual accountability, but that requires constant re-negotiation and consent, not external enforcement.

The promise of a covenantal polity for the unity and mission of the church

In spite of the perils of a covenantal polity identified above, I believe that such a polity holds great promise for promoting the unity of the church and enabling its mission in the world.

Covenantal polity and the unity of the church: The receptions of Faith and Order texts like BEM and the COCU Consensus demonstrate the difficulty of reconciling beliefs about church order and ministry. But in the actual practices of denominations in ordering their ministries, they are much more alike than their polities might predict. Though I do not know of sociological studies supporting that claim, I know that in my years of seminary teaching where the students came from many denominations, as I worked with them to help them prepare for ordination I discovered that whatever the official ecclesial polity might be, diverse church bodies and officials worked in a covenantal manner, seeking consensus among those involved in clergy placements or church disputes. All parties were consulted; every voice was heard; negotiation and consensus-building were the orders of the day, even if the official polity of the denomination mandates a different way of making binding decisions. Could we not hope for the day when practice would reshape theory, rather than practice having to ignore theory or having to deconstruct and reconstruct theory awkwardly?

Covenantal polity and the mission of the church: In the UCC and other mainline denominations, ecclesial discourse now centers on that word, mission, both as a requirement for church bodies to have a clear mission statement in postmodernity, where nothing about the church can be taken for granted; and mission as the way the church is to be in the world, with its message of good news and its vocation of extending compassion and working for justice for all people and for the creation. This emphasis on mission can be confusing to those who attach older meanings to missionary work and missionary societies, where missionaries were sent to make converts in cultures of traditional religions or other world religions. Today's missional emphasis is not that, but works to create partnerships across denominational and inter-religious lines to work together for just and peaceful societies.

The new emphasis on mission in post modernity is much more intensely local and personally engaging, or 'hands on' as many would express it. People with a strong sense of missional calling want to assist in those places where the hungry are being fed, where the poor are being clothed, where the prisoners can be visited, or to work in agencies and movements for justice, to overcome racism, to challenge white privilege, to improve public education, and to pass legislation that will make things better. Denominational mission giving, at the same time, suffers from its association with institutional religion where trust is diminished, and where the work of national mission boards seems far away. The exception to this rule seems to be mission trips to distant places, where people return transformed by the needs and opportunities they observed. But that is always a small number of all church members and participants.

What does a covenantal polity have to do with this new missional emphasis? Just this: a covenantal belief and practice in church governance can facilitate personal and local initiative, nurturing creative missional programs in local communities and in regions based on information closer at hand and based on a firmer grasp of local political possibilities. In a covenantal polity such missional initiatives need the understanding and support of wider denominational agencies; they do not need competitive efforts by such agencies.

Covenantal polity and post-modernity: I have referred to the cultural situation in the West as post-modernity, one aspect of which is its anti-institutionalism. It is not surprising, especially in the millennial generation, that institutions have fallen out of favor. All institutions appear corrupt and corrupting, religious, governmental, business and finance, educational, military, health care and the rest. Lust for power, greed, and personal aggrandizement appear to have replaced motives like serving the public good. Churches are not exempt from these charges, and as a result, church reform and renewal efforts join the anti-institutional chorus by preferring ecclesial language defining the church as a movement or beloved community rather than an institution. The two new kinds of churches in the West, Emergent Churches (cf. Marti and Ganiel 2015; the authors are sociologists sympathetic with the Emergent Church) and Mega-Churches, are predictably anti-institutional, in the sense of rejecting institutional aspects of traditional denominations, while having to manage their own institutional realities without falling into the old traps. I am suggesting, in these concluding remarks, that something like the covenantal polity of the United Church of Christ, may allow Christian renewal movements to reframe governance in a similar way, as forming prayerful covenants with God and one another to manage the affairs of old and new ecclesial institutions without making governance, or polity, an end in itself, and without removing polity from the realm of spiritual life, where it indeed belongs, not as some necessary but alien activity.

Abbreviations and bibliography

UCC United Church of Christ in the USA.
COCU Consultation on Church Union.
BEM Baptism, Eucharist and Ministry. Faith and Order Paper 111. Geneva: WCC 1982.

Bendroth, Margaret. 2015. The Last Puritans. Chapel Hill: The University of North Carolina Press.

Gunnemann, Louis H. 1977. The Shaping of the United Church of Christ. Cleveland Ohio: United Church Press.

Marti, Gerardo, and Gladys Ganiel. 2015. Deconstructing the Church. Understanding Emerging Christianity. Oxford: Oxford University Press.

LIST OF AUTHORS

The Rev. Klaas-Willem de Jong PhD LLM (1961) is an Assistant Professor of Church Polity and Manager of the Project 'The Dynamics of the Classical Reformed Liturgy in the Netherlands' at the PThU (Amsterdam-Groningen). E: k.w.de.jong@pthu.nl

The Rev. Hélène Evers PhD LLM (1965) serves the Sionskerk in Zwolle as a minister of the Protestant Church in the Netherlands (PKN). She is lecturer in Church Law at the Evangelical Theological Faculty (ETF) Louvain, Belgium, and President of the Standing Committee on Church Order of the PKN. E: Evers14@hetnet.nl

The Rev. Barry Ensign-George PhD serves as Coordinator for Theology and Worship in the Presbyterian Church (U.S.A.), E: barry.ensign-george@pcusa.org

The Rev. Daniel Griswold PhD is Coordinator and Stated Clerk of Holland Classis (RCA), having pastored churches in New York and Texas for 18 years. He received a Ph. D. in religious studies from Southern Methodist University.

The Rev. Allan Janssen PhD is Affiliate Professor of Theological Studies emeritus, New Brunswick Theological Seminary; General Synod Professor emeritus, Reformed Church in America. E: aljanssen@hotmail.com

Prof. Leo J. Koffeman (1948) is Professor Emeritus of Church Polity and Ecumenism at the PThU (Amsterdam), and an Extraordinary Professor at the University of Stellenbosch and the University of Pretoria (South Africa). E: ljkoffeman@pthu.nl

Prof. Leepo Modise is an Associate Professor in Systematic Theology at the University of South Africa. E: modislj@unisa.ac.za

The Rev. Basimane Makoko is a minister of the Word and Sacraments in URCSA Thabong East and PhD student in the Systematic theology (Supervised by Prof Leepo Modise) University of South Africa. E: revmakoko2@gmail.com

Prof. Nelus Niemandt (1957) is Professor in Mission Studies and Head of the Department Religion Studies at the University of Pretoria. He served as moderator of the General Synod of the Dutch Reformed Church in South Africa for two terms. E: nelusn@gmail.com

The Rev. Kathy Smith is Associate Director of the Calvin Institute of Christian Worship, Adjunct Professor of Church Polity at Calvin Theological Seminary, and Adjunct Professor of Congregational and Ministry Studies at Calvin University (Grand Rapids, Michigan, USA). E: kss4@calvinseminary.edu

The Rev. Herman A. Speelman PhD (1953) is Research Fellow in Early Modern Church History at the Theological University of Kampen and guest lecturer at the Roman Catholic Seminary Bovendonk in the diocese of Breda. E: haspeelman@tukampen.nl

Prof. Clyde Steckel is Professor Emeritus of Theology at the United Theological Seminary of the Twin Cities, in St. Paul, Minnesota, USA. He was also Academic Vice President and Dean at United. E: steckelcj@msn.com.

The Rev. Roy A. Surjanegara (1979) is a minister of the Gereja Kristen Indonesia, currently serving as a pastor in an Indonesian congregation within the Uniting Church of Australia (Perth). E: royassure@gmail.com

The Rev. Leon van den Broeke PhD is Associate Professor Religion, Law and Society/Church Polity and Chair of the Centre for Religion and Law at the Vrije Universiteit Amsterdam, and Associate Professor Church Polity and Director of the Deddens Church Polity Centre at the Theologische Universiteit Kampen, the Netherlands.

Church Polity and Ecumenism

Global Perspectives

edited by Prof. Dr. Leo J. Koffeman (Amsterdam), Prof. Dr. Allan J. Janssen (New Brunswick/USA), Prof. Dr. Johannes Smit (Potchefstroom/South Africa and Dr. C. Leon van den Broeke (Amsterdam)

Arjan Plaisier; Leo Koffeman (Eds.)

The Protestant Church in the Netherlands: Church Unity in the 21st Century

Stories and Reflections

This volume marks the tenth anniversary of the Protestant Church in the Netherlands on May 1st 2014. It outlines the long history that preceded the unification and the developments that occurred during the first decade of its existence. Further authors from other countries – Belgium, the United Kingdom, South Africa, and Australia – share the stories of their united churches. Their contributions enrich the picture of what church unification may entail. Thus the volume contributes to the field of ecumenical theology. Finally theologians from different backgrounds share some reflections on issues that these articles raise.

Bd. 4, 2014, 152 S., 29,90 €, br., ISBN 978-3-643-90530-7

Leo J. Koffeman; Johannes Smit (Eds.)

Protestant Church Polity in Changing Contexts II

Case Studies. Proceedings of the International Conference, Utrecht, The Netherlands, 7 – 10 November, 2011

Church polity as a theological discipline has become increasingly aware of the challenge of contextuality, due to secularization in the global North and a renewed awareness of inherited cultural and religious traditions in the global South. The ecumenical movement offers a particular framework for reflection on such developments.

This second conference volume presents thirteen case studies, from five continents, and covering church polity issues from perspectives like practical theology, civil law, and missiology. Another volume presents a number of ecclesiological and historical reflections.

Bd. 3, 2014, 208 S., 29,90 €, br., ISBN 978-3-643-90311-2

Allan J. Janssen; Leo Koffeman (Eds.)

Protestant Church Polity in Changing Contexts I

Ecclesiological and Historical Contributions. Proceedings of the International Conference, Utrecht, The Netherlands, 7 – 10 November, 2011

Church polity as a theological discipline has become increasingly aware of the challenge of contextuality, due to tendencies like secularization in the global North and a renewed awareness of inherited cultural and religious traditions in the global South. The ecumenical movement offers a particular framework for reflection on such developments.

This first conference volume contains studies in the fields of ecclesiology, church history, missiology, inter-cultural theology and practical theology. A second volume presents a number of case studies.

Bd. 2, 2014, 216 S., 29,90 €, br., ISBN 978-3-643-90310-5

Leo J. Koffeman

In Order to Serve

An Ecumenical Introduction to Church Polity

Ecclesiology is in the center of current ecumenical dialogue. However, this hardly seems to influence theological reflection on church polity. This book explores new avenues in this respect, in an attempt to enhance a truly ecumenical and inter-cultural approach of the theological discipline of church polity, without neglecting its juridical character. Key issues like liturgy and ordained ministry are featured, as well as concepts like missional church, synodality, episcopacy, and many others. Examples from Roman Catholic and Anglican canon law as well as from a number of Protestant church orders clarify the issues at stake. Finally, its contextual approach stimulates new reflection on church – state relationships. Does a deeper ecumenical understanding of the nature and mission of the church foster a renewal of church polity?

Bd. 1, 2014, 288 S., 29,90 €, br., ISBN 978-3-643-90318-1

LIT Verlag Berlin – Münster – Wien – Zürich – London

Auslieferung Deutschland / Österreich / Schweiz: siehe Impressumsseite